The Real Coco Chanel

To my mum, for our 6.00 am coffee chats and for this adventure we fearlessly started together so many years ago.

The Real Coco Chanel

Rose Sgueglia

WHITE
OWL

First published in Great Britain in 2020 by
White Owl
An imprint of
Pen & Sword Books Ltd
Yorkshire – Philadelphia

ISBN 978 1 52676 101 9

Typeset by Mac Style
Printed and bound in the UK by TJ International Ltd,
Padstow, Cornwall.

Pen & Sword Books Limited incorporates the imprints of Atlas,
Archaeology, Aviation, Discovery, Family History, Fiction, History,
Maritime, Military, Military Classics, Politics, Select, Transport,
True Crime, Air World, Frontline Publishing, Leo Cooper, Remember
When, Seaforth Publishing, The Praetorian Press, Wharncliffe
Local History, Wharncliffe Transport, Wharncliffe True Crime
and White Owl.

For a complete list of Pen & Sword titles please contact

PEN & SWORD BOOKS LIMITED
47 Church Street, Barnsley, South Yorkshire, S70 2AS, England
E-mail: enquiries@pen-and-sword.co.uk
Website: www.pen-and-sword.co.uk

Or

PEN AND SWORD BOOKS
1950 Lawrence Rd, Havertown, PA 19083, USA
E-mail: Uspen-and-sword@casematepublishers.com
Website: www.penandswordbooks.com

Contents

Acknowledgements

To Jeffie Pike Durham, thank you for sharing your mum's stories with me and for telling me about those wonderful times she had with Coco. Listening to your amazing tales from across the ocean has been a true gift which will stay with me forever.

To the team at the Pen & Sword for all the support and help and for answering my millions of questions.

To the Mary Evans Picture Library for the cover of this book and for the beautiful inside pictures.

To art historian and curator Gabriella Belli, who is currently director of the Foundation for the Municipal Museums of Venice for her time and for sharing with me her knowledge of the Culture Chanel exhibition.

To David Lubin, author of *Shooting Kennedy: JFK and The Culture of Images,* for sharing with me his thoughts on icons, myths and that famous Chanel pink suit.

To the London College of Fashion UAL for its striking pictures from the exhibition Coco Chanel: A New Portrait by Marion Pike (2013) which was held at the Fashion Space Gallery, London College of Fashion UAL; and to Daniel Caulfield-Sriklad for taking such brilliant pictures.

To Elisabetta Barisoni, head of Ca' Pesaro, and everyone at the Foundation for the Municipal Museums of Venice for being so lovely and helpful.

To everyone at Pushkin Press for all their support with the Paul Morand quotes.

To the House of Chanel for inspiring us all and for keeping the myth of Coco alive for all these years. And finally, to my family and friends for everything.

Preface

Before I wrote this book, I really thought I knew who Coco Chanel was.

I remember I had this clear image in my head of a woman who was bitter, insufferable and probably not very pleasant to have been around.

But as I started to write, I discovered a very different Coco – a smart businesswoman who made a strong contribution to the world of the arts. I found a woman who, excuse me for mentioning another heroine of mine, made in a very Beyoncé manner, lemonade out of lemons. With the lemons, in question, being privation, poverty and the death of those she loved the most.

By researching and writing about Coco, it struck me that the way she created an almost instant intimacy with the artists, politicians and personalities of her time would be a very difficult thing to achieve today. She lived in a world where connections were made in the warmth of a bohemian flat not whilst looking at a cold screen; a world which made me nostalgic and eager to learn more.

Through my research, I discovered that Coco was actually incredibly shy and sensitive. And she was drawn to all things mystical. It is this little-known side of her personality that I was eager to uncover. In this biography, I tried to have a look at Coco, her friends, her universe and how she so majestically succeeded in living the life of the perfect romantic heroine with all the wonders and the horrors that this brought. With each chapter, I have grown fonder of her. She was, after all, someone who was not afraid to take risks and she learnt everything she knew about being a designer on her own.

In one of her conversations with her friend, writer Paul Morand, she said:

'What did I know about my new profession? Nothing. I didn't know dressmakers existed. Did I have any idea of the revolution that I was about to stir up in clothing? By no means. One world was ending, another was about to be born. I was in the right place: an opportunity beckoned; I took it. I had grown up with this new century: I was therefore, the one to be consulted about its sartorial style. What were needed were simplicity, comfort and neatness: unwittingly, I offered all of that. True success is inevitable.'

I can hardly believe how successful she was. She just saw an opportunity and grabbed it, found a way to make it work and for this, she will always have my deepest admiration.

She also had the most fascinating life. She was the woman who had Stravinsky as her lover and Misia Sert as a best friend. She made costumes for the Ballet Russes and then created the most feminine fragrance ever conceived. She fell in love once, twice and then once more but every relationship had its purpose, its soul.

And then I found a woman who had the most delicate soul, something that I only learnt after talking to Jeffie Pike Durham, one of the most interesting women I have ever met, and the daughter of painter Marion Pike.

From my research, I found that Coco was a smart woman who dared to use her connections to get where she wanted and she got lucky, successful and rich whilst doing that. She moved on, left her past behind and eventually, started to live off her work.

The trouble was that Coco did not stop there. She became a patron, she supported artists, mainly men, financially, and that gave her power and an authority which was not in tune with the highly patriarchal society of the time. The establishment started mocking her, calling her names – one day she was a prostitute or a cocotte, and the next she was a drug addict.

It was like the world did not know what to do with her, what to do with her work, with her personality, and with her unbelievable confidence. Despite being so shy, as she was often described, she had a strength, a self-assurance that not many owned at the time. To see a woman succeed like that must have been difficult, especially for her lovers who tried to own her (Balsan), convince her that she was not enough (Capel) or get her to give up her business (Westminster).

And, lastly, when everyone thought they had seen the last of Mademoiselle Chanel, she came back. She had the courage to put her talent, her skills, and her taste to the service of women, once again.

Many have written about Coco and many still will, hopefully, one day, we will be able to find letters from her, telling us about her life, about her thoughts more or maybe just about her famous mysticism. I cannot help but wonder what she would think of the fashion world today, and what her thoughts would be on the current Chanel house. What would Coco think perhaps of the post-Karl Lagerfeld Chanel and what would she do differently?

Coco Chanel was many things, a romantic heroine, a designer, a lover, and a socialite, a woman of passions and secrets but who was she?

Who was the real Coco Chanel?

That is exactly what I have tried to find out.

Chapter 1

Coco Chanel, the Romantic Heroine

An almost imperceptible hint of Chanel N°5 scents the air of the Ritz Paris suite. Resting on the sofa, draped in a statement black dress with a double string of white pearls at her neck, Gabrielle Bonheur Chanel poses in a photograph taken in 1937 by Jean Moran.

She looks like someone from a bygone era, maybe Cleopatra taking a break or, perhaps, Emma Bovary emotionally crushed by a wave of 'ennui'. You might almost tiptoe quietly in the room where the photo is taken so as not to break the stillness of the moment and wake her up while in the back of your mind, a theory starts to unravel, is this just another act? Coco wore as many hats as she made in her first millinery shop in rue Cambon in Paris. She was the first designer to shorten skirts and offer women a different, more unorthodox approach to clothes.

She was the creative mind behind Chanel N°5 and a muse, an inspiration and a patron to intellectuals and artists who thrived thanks to her protection, love and financial help. She was also a Nazi spy – cold, precise and impeccably dressed, or was she? She had love affairs, one with a German officer, and several biographers have speculated that having such powerful relationships would have granted her full access to some of the most restricted areas during the occupation of Paris.

Yet her most important 'hat' to this day remains the one she ingeniously crafted for herself, a role only she played so well – the romantic heroine.

Saumur, a little town in the South of France, set the scene for Coco's narrative and gave her the background she needed to embroider her own story, something she would tell and re-tell her entire life. This medieval town, which overlooked both the Loire and the Thouet rivers, was nicknamed by many as 'the pearl of Anjou' for its beautiful scenery and thriving market which flourished during the Belle Époque.

It's here that Coco was born on a hot August night in 1883. Her first house was a poor, one-bedroom apartment where her mother gave birth on the kitchen table. Her father, Albert Chanel, was not present at the birth and Coco was registered two days later as 'Gabrielle', a name she never liked, and 'Chasnel' a misspelling of her surname.

Albert was a tradesman in his late twenties, and he travelled all over France for his business of buttons, fabrics, bonnets and wine. He came from a family of street vendors but had little success at his trade. His own mother was the daughter of a wealthy man but had renounced a life of luxury to run away with Albert's father, Henri.

Albert was a young ambitious salesman when he met Coco's mother, 19-year-old Eugenie Jeanne Devolle who was known as Jeanne. She was the sister of Albert's landlord Marin. Jeanne worked as a laundry woman but hoped, one day, to train as a seamstress just like her own mother before her. In his biography *Coco Chanel*, Madsen reported that Albert, Jeanne and their five children moved several times from Courpiere to Samur, Aubenas, Issoire and then to Samur again, as Albert tried to make a name for himself as a vendor.

In one of the rare times she talked about her father, Coco defined him as being 'an itinerant street vendor who peddled work clothes and undergarments, living a nomadic life, travelling to and from market towns, while the family resided in rundown lodgings.'

Changing cities, her father's instability and her mother's delicate health had a deep impact on Coco's personality and she grew up to be a lonely, sensitive child.

Despite the presence of her sisters, Julie and later Antoinette, who for her sweet disposition became her favourite, and her younger brothers, Alphonse and Lucien, she often played on her own. It's from those early childhood moments that she started to take sanctuary in her own reality, a world she had created for herself.

She was fascinated by cemeteries, she brought flowers, cutlery and anything she could find in the house to the graves of strangers.

She would spend hours speaking to the deceased at their gravesides, something which not surprisingly alarmed her mother who forced her to stop. She once said to her good friend, writer Claude Delay, how much she did not like the idea of the family. Later in her life, she paid off her brothers and pretended they had never existed.

When Coco was 10, her mother decided to return to Samur. Exhausted by the many pregnancies and tired from having to run after her husband from one place to another, Jeanne had developed a respiratory disease which frequently left her feeling tired and dizzy. Her husband joined the family occasionally, as he had fathered another child outside the marriage and took on his nomadic lifestyle again. After the last pregnancy weakening her body and the trauma of losing the child in infancy, Jeanne drew her last breath in 1895.

Speaking about her mother's death, Coco, who was always very reserved and careful on the topic, said to a friend: 'Since my earliest childhood I have been certain that they have taken everything away from me, that I am dead. I knew that when I was twelve. You can die more than once in your life.'

After Jeanne's death, Albert took off, leaving the boys with farmers to become child workers and subjecting them to years of abuse and neglect. He left the girls at an orphanage run by nuns at Aubazine near Brive-la-Gallairde. Coco and her siblings never saw him again. That is when Coco's life took a turn for the worse as she found herself abandoned by her father and separated from her younger brothers. All of a sudden, at 12 years old, the icon, the legend and the romantic heroine became an orphan.

Chapter 2

Chanel, the Orphan

You can almost feel the cold air of the morning as it lingers on your skin.

A little girl with deep black eyes is left outside the steps of a tall building, her sister, maybe younger, is with her; as a nun opens the door, as her father leaves on his cart without turning back. The nun becomes two, then three and then, we finally realise that the little girl and her sister have been abandoned, left to their destiny by their family, in the care of a secluded orphanage.

Coco Avant Chanel (in English, *Coco Before Chanel*) is a 2009 film which has the merit of showing Mademoiselle Coco before she became a brand and a style icon. The movie explores those early moments in Gabriel Bonheur Chanel's life when she first came in touch with all the brutality in the world. She had just lost her mother after a long illness, and her father had absconded from all his parental responsibilities. To find herself an orphan at such a young age must have been terrifying for the young Coco.

The pain of being left behind and finding herself on her own, despite the presence of her sisters, Julia who was 13 and Antoinette who was eight at the time, was, later described by Gabrielle herself to one of her closest friends, the French author Paul Morand (1976):'I threw my arms around my father's neck. "Take me away from here. Now, now, my dear Coco, everything will be all right, I will be back, I'll take you with me, we'll have a home again…" 'Those were his last words. He didn't come back. I never lived under my father's roof again. He occasionally wrote and told me to trust him and said that his business was doing well. And then that was all: we never heard another word from him.'

Known for her stories as much as her designs, there is a chance that Gabrielle had already started fabricating her intricate web of lies even then at the age of 12, and there is an even better chance that this last meeting with Albert, her father, had never really occurred. The orphanage, she would call home for the following six years, was far less colourful than the one she would, often, describe in her made-up romantic stories.

It was 1895 and there was no trace of romance as Gabrielle began one of the most dramatic chapters in her life; a chapter which brought her to Aubazine, a remote orphanage in the heart of the Corrèze.

Surrounded by a forest and stone-built, the monastery turned orphanage, with its white walls and big black doors, provided endless inspiration to Gabrielle's narrative and gave her the beginning she needed for the performance of her life, the role of the romantic heroine. Hidden behind the strong branches of the Aubazine forest, the orphanage could not have been more secluded, and it certainly amplified a deep sense of abandonment in a young Gabrielle. As she learnt how to cope not only with the void left by her mother and her father's betrayal but also with the separation from her younger brothers Lucien and Alphonse, she felt like a cruel destiny had taken everything she loved and cared for. Gabrielle's brothers did not join their sisters at Aubazine as the orphanage only accepted girls and both boys were sent to a local farm to become child labourers.

The practice of sending orphans to work with local farmers was common throughout the nineteenth century with many children becoming child labourers in France and starting to work in the fields. When not taken into care by local orphanages, girls, like Gabrielle and her sisters, were, also, sent away to be trained as servants for the most affluent families. With the advent of the Industrial Revolution and the creation of factories throughout France, the demand for extra labour became more and more pressing and soon impoverished children were being exploited all over France. They represented a profitable, as well as, an easy target for employers and they were, often, mistreated, underpaid and forced to work longer hours than adults. Due to their smaller stature, they were, often, used to complete difficult tasks that adults could not. At this time, there were still not enough laws safeguarding children and banning child labour, and orphan children became a prime target for merciless employers.

Many children were placed with foster families who survived on their small salary and took advantage of their labour in the fields or, later, in the factories.

Gabrielle's brothers sadly became part of this mass exploitation. It was nothing short of a semi-slavery as they had to work in the field for long hours under the hot sun, and not surprisingly, several children, especially the youngest ones, perished from malnourishment and neglect. Alphonse and Lucien were children, boys of that time, who had been failed by the new French society, a society which was still affected by the echoes of the French Revolution. The king and his family had been gone for quite some time yet those ideals of liberté, égalité and fraternité still only applied to the richest with both the church and the nobility maintaining their privileges as well as a prominent role over the peasants or third state who were forced to work for them with no or little salary.

Despite a century of distance, the French Revolution was still influencing members of society as the rebellious movement had changed rules and conventions as well as overthrowing all the institutions of the past. It was a confusing moment for France as a whole and Gabrielle and her siblings found themselves growing up in the middle of both the chaos and the change.

While her younger (Lucien and Alphonse were respectively nine and five at the time) brothers faced child labour as well as being sold to foster parents who forced them to work every day, often under extreme circumstances, Gabrielle had to confront a whole other level of abuse. Her world offered far more comfort than the one her brothers were experiencing yet she found it difficult to appreciate her condition; despite her and her sisters being spared a life of work from a young age, she found it challenging to rejoice of her stay and find a little light in her new life at Aubazine.

The orphanage stood far away from everything she knew and loved, it made her feel claustrophobic because of its stillness: she was the daughter of a tradesman who had dragged his family throughout the South of France for over a decade, that was all she had ever known and now missed. During those years spent at Aubazine, she also experienced jealousy and frustration for the very first time in her life. The Aubazine orphanage was a place specifically conceived for helping children from the most disadvantaged backgrounds, however it also worked as a boarding school for a small, more exclusive elite; these children had affluent parents who would regularly contribute to the orphanage with generous donations and for this reason, could enjoy a much better living situation at Aubazine.

Dreading the comparison with these girls and envying how highly regarded they were by the nuns, Gabrielle decided to start to lie about her past: in her, always, flowing, romantic narrative, she too became a little Mademoiselle from a family of means, not abandoned but just left to a better, more sophisticated education. The rich girls slept in softer, bigger beds, their breakfast was better and their whole Aubazine experience was infinitely superior to the one Gabrielle and her sisters, who often slept in cold rooms, had to endure. However, in her stories, Gabrielle never let herself or her siblings feel inferior; her exceptionally well-fabricated narrative took a life of its own, she told those who dared ask about her parents that her father could not be a more positive and luminous presence in their life.

At Aubazine, she started telling everyone that Albert was a successful businessman who travelled so much for work, he had a job so fascinating that would often take him far away on remote, exotic trips to the United States; she told everyone that even though he would have loved nothing more than taking care of his girls, he had to do, quite reluctantly, what was best for them and leave them at Aubazine where he knew they would have a good education. She always made sure to mention how devoted he was and how he never failed to bring her and her sisters a present every time he visited.

The pain of being discarded so carelessly by the second most important parental figure she had known had a deep impact on the intricate web of lies she so expertly crafted. At Aubazine, she didn't let her condition of being an orphan define who she was, that was just another label, a hat she did not care for and, most importantly, had no intention of wearing. It just did not fit with who she was and most importantly, with who she wanted to be; and despite being only 12, she started to recognise that in order to move on with her life, she had to give some direction to her own narrative, hence the web of lies. It was not like she was not familiar with the truth, and she was not in any way delusional. At 12-years-old, Gabrielle Chanel was grounded, aware of her status and determined to do something in order to change it.

Separated by both her parents and part of her family, Gabrielle started to develop a strong individualism and to distinguish herself from the other girls at Aubazine, including her own sisters. She was a smart girl who craved the freedom of her early childhood and was not lacking in pride. At the orphanage, there was very little patience with proud girls and especially during the first years, Gabrielle's pride did not do her any favours. She rejected Aubazine, the nuns' obsolete rules, all their praying, catechism and religion, and then she rejected the nuns themselves. Despite becoming very spiritual in her own way, with a predisposition for anything mystical and mysterious, later in her life, Gabrielle did not like religion; and she did not answer to being told what to do and how to do it. She did not like to kneel and soon she started to make up stories to tell the priest in confession, and this certainly did not find the approval of the nuns and their community at Aubazine.

Later in her life, when she had already made a name for herself in the fashion world, she would refuse to acknowledge both the orphanage and the nuns. She told Paul Morand that she was raised by 'aunts' and not nuns. She did not completely ignore Aubazine and the presence of an orphanage in her past but she said that it was not something that she had experienced first-hand; her sisters had, in fact, been sent to a convent but not her, as she was made of a more sensitive disposition that could not have survived in such a strict environment. Despite changing names and locations, the 'aunts' were no different from the nuns at Aubazine.

She detested everything about the aunts and said to Paul Morand: 'I say no to everything, because of a fierce-too fierce-love of life, because of a need to be loved, because everything about aunts irritates and upsets me. Horrible aunts!'

She must have realised that she had gone too far in being so vocal about her hatred towards the aunts and tried to rectify this but didn't quite succeed:

> 'Adorable aunts', she said now, always to Morand. 'They belonged to that peasant bourgeoise that never sets foot in town, or in their village, unless driven there by bad weather, for the winter, but which never loses touch with the earth that feeds them. Horrible aunts for whom love is a luxury and childhood a sin.'

The nuns or the aunts, as she liked to call them, were strict, imposed rules and did not tolerate anyone disobeying or defying their rules as Aubazine had stood on a secular tradition of rigour and conformity for many centuries.

The Aubazine Abbey and, consequently the orphanage, was founded by two pious and devoted young men in 1125, Stephen and Pierre. They quickly had met the approval of the local community and built two monasteries, one for men and one for women, Stephen became their official founder as Saint Stephen of Aubazine or Saint Etienne in France and established a group of monks devoted to prayer and study who found in the tranquillity of the forest their inspiration and call. He also served as an abbot and later joined the Cistercians order, a Catholic religious order of monks and nuns that followed the rules of Saint Benedict, an even stricter order which had Stephen and his monks take the three Benedictine rules of stability, fidelity to the monastic way of life, and obedience. Several centuries later, Aubazine became renowned for offering sanctuary to those in need; suppressed during the French Revolution, the monastery was then seized in 1791 while the abbey survived and turned into a pivotal centre, and even granted refuge to Jewish people escaping the Holocaust during the Second World War. In 1890, much closer to Gabrielle's orphanage years, the nuns of the Saint-Coeur de Marie opened an orphanage with thirty-five places, with this ancient order of nuns making it their mission to take care of the poor and rejected.

Gabrielle did not like the nuns and she often said that the nuns did not like her back. She kept mostly to herself, spending time on her own and avoiding them as much as she could; often acting spoiled and difficult on purpose, like the first time they met.

'My aunts had already had dinner, we had not,' she said to Morand. They were surprised that people who had travelled all day had not had anything to eat. That disturbed their programme and their frugality, but they finally overcame their stark provincial rigidity and regretfully said, "We will make you two soft-boiled eggs."'

Coco was hungry and loved eggs, but she had already decided that she was not going to like the aunts and their arrogance, and to make sure they understood how much she disliked them, she decided not to eat. Far more than a little girl's tantrum, this could be seen as yet another refusal to be abandoned to her new life with the aunts or nuns at Aubazine.

Provinciality was, also, a recurring theme in Gabrielle's stories, she could not stand the idea of dealing with someone or, let alone, being accused of being provincial and having a closed mind; that was a mood, an arrogance and a sense of superiority, she believed, that came with living always in the same location or province, repeating the same activities day after day, and believing to hold the key to any truth in the world. Despite her challenging relationship with the nuns, Gabrielle often admitted that she felt she still owed part of her success to Aubazine. As much as she detested that world, she found in Aubazine the starting point she needed in life, as up until joining the orphanage, Gabrielle and her sisters had not spoken the national language. French was exclusively spoken by children from the most affluent families, as these were the only ones who could afford an education, let alone books. Gabrielle, her sisters and her family spoke a local dialect. That is probably why many writers make the assumption that Gabrielle did not feel comfortable enough writing in French. However, there could be several reasons explaining why still today, we haven't found many letters from Chanel.

It might have been challenging to keep track of the infinite childhood versions she had made up her whole life and maybe she just preferred not to leave anything permanent on paper. Another hypothesis could have something to do with later speculation that Gabrielle worked as a spy under the Nazi regime; if that was the case, she wouldn't leave any proof in writing. Despite never becoming an avid letter writer, Aubazine gave her the education she needed to get an acceptable start in life with a basic, general knowledge of everything she needed from mathematics to French. Yet, the most precious skill Gabrielle learnt at Aubazine was sewing; at first, she tried simple things like hems on the sheets for her own trousseaux clothes and linen collected by young girls for their future marriage.

Aubazine proved to be beneficial and Gabrielle found herself enjoying some of the aspects of the life there; she was particularly taken by how clean and simple everything always seemed to look, with fresh, clean linens piled in cupboards and the smell of soap leaving a long-lasting impression in her memory. She was really taken by Aubazine's cleanliness and simplicity and later in her life, she tried to recreate that feeling with her designs. All the orphans followed a strict daily routine made up mostly of early mass and prayers, they had to attend mandatory classes and were often brought to hike through the woods.

Gabrielle might have refused Aubazine and everything it stood for but its rigour crept into her being and inspired her life, fashion and career. A clear example is how the intricate work of the glasses of the ceiling of the Aubazine Abbey gave her the idea for her iconic trademark as well as for some of her most beautiful jewellery designs. At one point in her life, she would also learn to be a little nicer yet still slightly bitter towards the aunts, as she started to recognise their deep and overall positive impact on her life: 'I have been ungrateful towards the odious aunts. I owe them everything. A child in revolt becomes a person with armour and strength. It's the kisses, caresses, teachers and vitamins that kill children and turn them into unhappy or sickly adults.'

Later in her life, Gabrielle added more and more fictional details to her experience at Aubazine. During interviews or even when talking to her closest friends, Gabrielle omitted Aubazine when mentioning her past, she didn't only refuse to call the nuns by any other names but aunts but also maintained a well-elaborated farce. She pretended that, despite her father's abandonment, she had been the one kept within the family walls and not raised as an orphan. During those conversations, she would also often contradict herself; sometimes she would absolve Albert of any guilt and would pretend that he had written to her during those long years of separation, telling her all about his wonderful travels and the amazing people he had met. Other times, when she was probably too tired of the lies, she reluctantly admitted the truth: Albert had never written or visited her, she had left Gabrielle and her siblings on their own, starting a new family and having other children somewhere else in the world. When she was not lying about him, she always showed compassion and empathy towards him and seemed tolerant of his flaws. Often, she said that she didn't blame him for leaving his family behind, she didn't hold any grudge and that she would have had done exactly the same thing if she could have.

Despite absolving her father, she was way harsher towards her extended family and could hardly hide her resentment that her relatives had not taken care of her and her siblings when they had needed them the most. When she would talk about provinciality, she would not only criticise the nuns, as they lived confined in their little convent far from anything in the world, but also her extended family, particularly from her father's side; those who had abandoned her to her destiny, without realising they were setting her up for grandeur.

Gabrielle's extended family from her father's side included her grandparents and her two aunts, Louise Coster and Adrienne Chanel, who she was relatively close to.

Louise was married and had no children of her own and that is why she seemed, at least at first, to take an interest in the Chanel sisters. She was particularly taken by Gabrielle as they had a mutual love for hats. Louise was quite the milliner herself and enjoyed making hats for herself and her friends. She was the one who would push Gabrielle to be a bit more experimental with her sewing, inspiring her love for fashion and, particularly, accessories. Adrienne was her father's youngest sister and she was only one year older than Gabrielle, the two shared common interests including fashion and books, and truly enjoyed each other's company; they were so close in age that Adrienne became more a sister to Gabrielle than an aunt. Every summer, during the holidays, Gabrielle and her sisters spent time with their grandparents in Moulins and their aunts Louise and Adrienne in Varenne. Later, her grandparents decided to get Lucien and Alphonse back, freeing them from years of foster care and child labour and finding them employment as apprentices.

Despite her controversial relationship with her family, Gabrielle really enjoyed staying in Moulins and exploring its charming, artistic venues. Established in the year 990, Moulins had been the seat of the Duchy of Bourbon, from 1327 to 1527 and it showed evidence of the patronage of Peter II and Anne de France, under which the court had some of its most prosperous years boasting some of the most acclaimed Renaissance artists. Counting on five centuries of history from The Middle Ages to the Art Nouveau, Moulins was very dear to Gabrielle and a nice change of pace to Aubazine.

Aubazine was a quiet little island of tranquillity and peace. There was not much to do and Gabrielle would often escape the boredom of her days by finding refuge in books; these represented for Gabrielle the very first step towards the construction of her romantic narrative, the one that will always paint her as the tragic and romantic heroine of her own life. Often in her later conversations with friends and the media, she would mention an attic, a place where she could read and lose herself in those books; the attic, maybe just another room at Aubazine or a little place she would later share with Adrienne in Moulins, was a quiet refuge where she could read in peace. It was her sanctuary, her library, a place where she could read everything she wanted, a place where she found herself.

'We never bought books at home,' Gabrielle said to Morand. 'We cut out the serial from the newspaper and we sewed together those long sheets of yellow paper. That's what little Coco lapped up in secret, in the so-called attic. I copied down whole passages from novels I had read, which I would slip into my homework: "Where on earth did you get hold of all that?" The teacher asked me. Those novels taught me about life; the nourished my sensibility and pride. I have always been proud.'

Books and novels played a big part in Gabrielle's life, a love she brought with her during those long summers with her father's family in Moulins.

In Moulins, under the casual supervision of her grandparents, Gabrielle would share a room with Adrienne and together they would read secret romance novels published in instalments in newspapers, they were called feuilletons. Both Chanel girls loved those stories with one of them, The Two Little Vagrants, a story about poor girls who become rich ladies, becoming one of their favourites. Gabrielle also succeeded in often smuggling those stories into Aubazine, she was caught several times by her nuns and teachers but never gave up the pleasure of a good romantic read before going to bed.

Once she and her sisters were staying with her family when something interesting occurred. She had grown fond of the description of a romantic heroine from one of her books, a lady described as wearing a purple dress with ruffles; something in that passage really inspired Gabrielle and made her wish to own something exactly like that. She was a teenager, forced into a never-changing situation of neglect, who wished for an opportunity in life, and that is why she did something rather spontaneous and risky. While visiting her relatives, she managed to charm her aunts' seamstress into making her a replica of the same dress she had read about in her book, she never asked for her aunts' permission and never told them.

At the time, she was probably about 15 or 16. Once finished, she wore the dress with her ribbons and ruffles, took a twirl and paraded it for her aunts for the first time.

They were horrified at such audacity, but she was desperate to wear it to church, only her Aunt Louise took one look at her and just told her to go upstairs and change into something more appropriate. The purple dress was sent back to the seamstress who lost her business with the Chanel family.

Talking about the infamous dress, Coco said to Morand in one of their conversations:

> 'As a child, I had succumbed, like everyone else. In Mont-Dore, aged fifteen, I had been allowed to order a dress of my choice: my dress was mauve as a bad novel published by Lemerre, laced at the back, as though I had had hundreds of maids, and with bunches of artificial Parma violets on each side, as in a play by Rostand; a collar held up by two stays that dug into my neck; below, at the back, a sweeping train with which to gather up all the sweethearts behind you.'

The disappointment for the loss of the purple dress soon found relief in one of the many novels or feuilletons she used to read in newspapers or magazines every day.

A young Gabrielle was particularly taken by the likes of Sibylle Riqueti de Mirabeau, known as Gyp, and her fascinating stories. Sibylle Aimee Marie Antoinette Gabrielle de Riquetti de Mirabeau was an acclaimed French writer who came from a noble family, her father was the great-grandson of Victor de Riquetti, marquis de Mirabeau and her mother a fellow writer for *Le Figaro*. Sibylle, who married a count and had three children, was brought up by her authoritarian grandfather in the love and nostalgia of Napoleonic France. She was the first woman to be vocal about how much she hated being a woman and she was also an only child; something that made her even more agreeable to Gabrielle, who several times, later in her life, wished she was an only child. Gabrielle was, particularly, inspired by Sibylle's works and public person; she represented an unusually independent woman, especially for the time, who was not afraid to express her opinions.

She was an anti-Semite, a right-wing activist and a Boulangiste (a specific type of French nationalist) working as part of a right-hand movement which was founded under General Boulanger between 1886 and 1889; and because of her opinions, she was the victim of several attempts on her life and one kidnap. Sibylle's works and novels including her comic sketches which criticised and humoured both society and politicians from the French Republic era gave her great fame in France and beyond.

Sibylle published almost a hundred works with one of her best being Le Mariage de Chiffon, a story about a young girl, Chiffon being forced to marry a military officer but falling in love with her stepfather's brother.

She was educated and unlike most women of her generations and much like Gabrielle herself, Sibylle had grown up resenting male authority and doing everything in her power to defy it.

Sibylle and Gabrielle shared more than just a name (Gabrielle was one of Sibylle's middle names), they both had a strong imagination and nurtured similar political ideas. Sibylle's work gave Gabrielle the motivation and inspiration she needed most during her most tragic years, the time spent at Aubazine, when the idea of playing the romantic heroine of her life started to take its initial form. Sibylle represented the heroine young Gabrielle aspired to be; she was from an aristocratic family, had a title and was not afraid to express her ideas despite violent often life-threatening repercussions. She also wrote about love and about young girls saying no to a life of luxury to chase love, yet she was also very vocal about her ideas of independence; no wonder, young Gabrielle grew up to be very taken by her world, aspiring one day to either fall in love like those book heroines she had read about or to give them a voice with her work. Sibylle was everything Gabrielle wanted to be admired, loved, envied yet with a dangerous allure, something she became later in her life when she dropped Gabrielle to become Coco.

Chapter 3

Coco Chanel

In her first photo modelling one of her own designs, she is wearing a big black and white hat, her eyes are shut and yet she is still managing to pose for the camera. This picture was taken in her first career as a hat designer. She was probably only in her early twenties, and she looks incredibly young and beautiful. Yet despite her youth, she exudes the aura of someone who knows where she is going and is confident that good fortune will find her.

It is not difficult to imagine what she might have thought as she left Aubazine behind – the place of all her torments, the orphanage where she had been left by Albert and where she had found herself increasingly detached from her sisters. Aubazine was a memory she would rather have forgotten, something she seemed to have no problem doing later in her life. Yet, she could hardly ignore that the orphanage was also the place where her romantic heroine narrative had found its own pace and finally begun to unravel.

Coco arrived in Moulins right in the middle of the Belle Époque, an era of quiet and creativity that spanned almost half a century, ending with the First World War. It was a time when anything seemed possible and it's not surprising that Coco wanted to take her part in such a vibrant, innovative period.

At the very beginning of the Belle Époque, France was still finding its feet after its bitter defeat in the Franco-Prussian war. Having lost so many patriots in the conflict, morale had been low, but the new dawn infused the population with the energy and motivation they needed to move forward again. The decade before the First World War was a time of incredible prosperity and beauty in France when the population grew by two-thirds and Paris became a city to be proud of; what with the creation of the Statue of Liberty for the Americans, and later, the erection of the Eiffel Tower. This was a time of enormous fun with the rise of cafes and entertainment venues like the Moulin Rouge, which quickly became famous for its scandalous dance routines, usually performed late at night. Change was everywhere, as lights, cameras and gramophones became widely available and it was that spirit of innovation that must have inspired Coco's designs.

Visual arts boomed during the Belle Époque era with the popularity of the art nouveau movement and fashion flourished too with designer Jeanne Paquin becoming famous whilst Coco was still a teenager, she was renowned for her marketing stunts as she sent models dressed in her designs to the races and then to the opera to get her work noticed.

Coco found herself in the vibrant city of Moulins as a young, unattached 18-year-old, right in the middle of all the noise created by the Belle Époque. Moulins was where her grandparents lived and where her beloved aunt Adrienne was also staying so it just made sense for her to move there too. Adrienne was probably the main attraction for Coco as the two of them were inseparable with their mutual love for books and romantic stories.

A different, less romantic path lay ahead for Coco's sisters. Julia, who had joined Coco in Moulins, ended up helping her grandparents at the market and falling in love with a tradesman while Antoinette, who was the youngest, stayed at Aubazine for a little while before joining Coco and helping her in her business ventures before marrying Edouard Fléming when she was in her thirties.

Antoinette was Coco's favourite sister, perhaps because she was the youngest of the family, someone she felt she needed to take care of. Julia, who never married, despite getting pregnant quite soon in her relationship, gave birth to a child, a little boy named André who was later adopted by Coco after his mother's tragic death.

Both the birth of André and the death of Julia are shrouded in mystery. Once Coco revealed that Julia had died of bronchitis yet many biographers believed that she had let herself die one night after rolling herself several times in the snow; the reason was that the tradesman, who reminded everyone of Albert and who Coco didn't like, had refused to marry her despite the pregnancy causing her to fall into a deep depression. The birth of André was also mysterious and many believe that it was not Julia but Coco who, unable to have an abortion as it was illegal at the time, had given birth to him and left the baby boy with her older sister; André would have been her only child.

Despite abortion being illegal, there was a practice in rural France at the time of performing abortions by smothering.

With her first lover Balsan, not being a father figure and abortion being illegal, Coco might have decided to give birth anyway and then leave the child with family, someone she trusted, someone like her sister; which could also explain why she decided to adopt the boy after Julia's death.

If Julia was a mystery, so were Coco's brothers Alphonse and Lucien who kept away from Coco and her glamorous world, as they were, at least at first, away labouring in the fields and then training at the market so as to continue the family tradition and become salesmen. Coco did not maintain a relationship with her brothers, and, in later conversations with her friends, she hardly ever mentioned any members of her family, let alone, Alphonse or Lucien. Once she was famous, a rumour began to circulate that she had paid them off to keep their distance and to never interfere in her business affairs or to give interviews, and much like the rest of the Chanel family, they became a vague memory.

Antoinette was the only family relationship Coco maintained with her siblings. She was the one she still saw once she'd become an acclaimed designer, partly because she truly cared for her and partly because her marriage to Fleming (a wealthy Canadian Royal Air command pilot) made her highly sought after in French society and someone not to be ashamed of. Sadly though, Antoinette died at only 33 – there were rumours that she committed suicide, although this was never verified.

Despite her family ties in Moulins, Coco felt free for the first time, far away from Aubazine, she was finally, almost, an independent woman capable of using everything she had learnt from her books to craft her own story. In Moulins, she and Adrienne quickly enrolled in a Catholic school, Notre Dame De Moulins, to continue their education and became employable. That is when she also decided to drop her full name; Gabrielle was too long and articulated and she was looking for something simple yet easily memorable. Later in her life, she made up several stories on why the final choice had been Coco. At first, she tried to give a warm, family-connected explanation; during several conversations and interviews, she often said that it had been her father, Albert, to be the first to call her Coco.

She was his little Coco, a pet name, an affectionate way to remind her of how much he really loved her and of how deeply he cared for her. She explained to her friends several times that her father had been away for business the day she was born and had not been able to choose an appropriate name for his little girl. Her real name, Gabrielle, was after the nun who had delivered her while Coco was the sweet one her father had specifically chosen for her.

Another, more plausible explanation was that Coco was the name given to her by some friends after seeing her perform, Qui qu'a vu coco; a popular French song which told the story of a young girl looking for her lost dog.

A further explanation, and probably the one Coco disliked the most, lies in the term 'cocotte', a woman of loose morals or in other words, a prostitute; cocottes were French entertainers who also worked as prostitutes and used to perform in France, in little cafes including the Folies and the Moulin Rouge between the end of 1800 and 1900.

Coco never publicly accepted this theory and always refused to identify herself as a cocotte, she often complained to her friends about how jealous people must have been of her to accuse her of such a horrible thing; according to her, the media was always after an easy, often defamatory, explanation. She strongly believed that she had been labelled a cocotte simply because people wanted to attribute all her success purely to luck rather than her hard work and talent as a designer. According to Mademoiselle Chanel, the only truth was that she had worked herself silly and that was the only reason behind her success. One last hypothesis, which stands as the most romanticised of them all attributes the creation of her name to Étienne Balsan, her first lover, who first called her Coco for the first time after seeing her perform in Moulins.

It matters very little where the name came from, the most important thing is that Gabrielle had left Aubazine, but it was Coco who embraced her new life in Moulins.

Coco was sent to the Notre Dame school in Moulins where she would complete her education. It was there that she learnt how to improve her sewing technique, something that quickly placed her and Adrienne in employment. They found work at a local store on the Rue de l'Horloge; the shop sold trousseaux for young women getting ready for marriage, mourning clothes to the local gentry and layettes for newborn babies.

Coco and Adrienne shared a little bedroom just above the shop, and usually on weekends, they would also work for a local tailor, altering breeches for cavalry officers; they both really enjoyed working there, as the vibe was completely different to the one at the store on the Rue de l'Horloge. Because of the two young girls, the tailor shop soon became exceptionally popular with local soldiers; and more and more officers started to come not only for their breeches to be fixed but also to invite the Chanel girls to attend nights out at a local pavilion called La Rotonde.

Coco and Adrienne, beautiful and young, were not exactly artists in the performing sense, yet they managed to conquer a regular spot at La Rotonde. They were singing on stage for the very first time and in order to improve their repertoire, they began to add a few new routines; these were *Ko Ko Ri Ko* and *Qui qu'a vu Coco?* the infamous song considered responsible for giving Coco her name.

The Chanel girls were among other girls called *poseuses*, they were performers who entertained the crowd before and after the performances of bigger stars. Although they both lacked the singing, dancing or even acting ability to make it as entertainers, performing at La Rotonde was still a good way to make themselves known to the artistic crowd and to mingle with some influential characters whilst earning some pocket money.

Later in her life, Coco never really acknowledged her past as a performer and she quickly dismissed any artistic background, as during the Belle Époque era, the confine between being a performer and a cocotte was always a little blurry and Coco did not want to be associated with any of that.

However, in 1906, Coco decided to take her performing career to a whole different level and decided to audition as a singer at the spa resort town of Vichy; she had hoped to get a spot on stage but her voice, being too weak, failed to secure her any more artistic work.

Famous since the Gallo-Roman period and renowned for its healing and therapeutic waters, Vichy was highly regarded by the likes of Napoleon III and Madame de Sévigné, it was a glamorous, highly sought-after place and it certainly managed to grasp the attention of young Coco with its active social life and vibrant residents.

As she still needed to work during the season and she didn't want to leave Vichy, she managed to secure a job as a *donneuse d'eau*, a simple yet interesting job where she had to hand glasses of the curative mineral water to the rich people coming for their season of self-care and wellbeing; this gave her the chance to network with some of the most affluent people of the time and to make the acquaintance of many high profile personalities.

Vichy fascinated Coco, she liked to watch the eccentric people parading their wealth and she was enchanted by their foreign accents; she must have wished to be one of them, a foreign heiress from a noble family enjoying the therapeutic, almost miraculous springs. She later told her friends that at Vichy, she had met businessman and, later, lover Étienne Balsan. In one of her long conversations with Morand, Coco said that she had met him whilst having tea with some aunts who had come and visited her while she was working in Vichy. The routine of having tea with her family was always a very important element in all Coco's stories, as she believed only ladies had tea and she so desperately wanted to be one of them. Coco was a great narrator, someone who could charm you with her voice and stories, so much so that it was hard to establish whether there was any truth in anything she said; there is a chance that her first meeting with Balsam was not in Vichy but in Moulins, many believe that the two met while she was performing at La Rotonde with Adrienne, as Balsan who was quite the socialite used to often attend such nights with his friends.

The meeting between Coco and Balsan is a pivotal moment in Coco's life, maybe her most important one; according to Coco's conversations with Morand, at Vichy, where they met, Balsan owned a racing stable, something that really caught Coco's attention, as she loved horses despite never having ridden in her life. She was also quite taken by Balsan, his lifestyle and all the endless possibilities a relationship with such a powerful man could bring her. She told Morand that during her first encounter with Balsan, the pair only exchanged a few words, but when she met him the following day, he invited her to visit him at his chateau after the summer in Compiègne.

When Coco came back from Vichy at the end of the season, she realised that she didn't have the talent to make a career out of performing, and so instead with no real prospect of a future, she decided to accept Balsan's invitation, and join him in Compiègne.

Compiègne was a little town of Roman origins which stood as part of the Oise area in the region of the Northern Hauts just along the Oise River. Often called Compendium, the city, which really boomed during the Middle Age, was a prestigious site for assemblies and councils during the time of the Merovingian kings and nurtured a true adoration for another romantic heroine, Joan of Arc, whose capture by the Burgundians in 1430 was commemorated with a monument. Compiègne was also well-known for its town hall which had a gothic structure and its beautiful churches that dated as far back as the thirteenth century and were dedicated to Saint Antoine and Saint Jacques.

The city's Catholic heritage resonated with Coco and at first, she thought it was a marvelous place. It was after all enchantingly steeped in history and the Compiègne Palace was one of its most beautiful attractions. Built in the eighteenth century by Louis XV, the palace was later restored by Napoleon I and became the scene for numerous historical events including the place where Napoleon first welcomed

Marie Louise of Austria, and Louis XVIII met Alexander I of Russia. It was also where the wedding of Leopold I, King of Belgians, to Marie-Louise of Orleans took place in 1832.

In many ways, Compiègne offered the perfect location for Coco's escape from Vichy, as she felt free for the first time ever. But in order to stop people from searching for her, she had to create an intricate web of lies.

She told her grandparents that, disillusioned with the performing arts world, she had finally decided to embrace her seamstress career and gone home, and she told her aunts that she had gone to her grandparents to take some time and have a think about her next move; no one checked on her, no one bothered to find out where she was staying, and no one, sadly enough, seemed to care.

Compiègne was her chance to figure out what she wanted to do with her life. Balsan, who had invited Coco, was shocked to find out that she had not only accepted his invitation but also planned to stay for quite some time. However, the two of them struck up a romantic relationship and a friendship which lasted for the rest of their life.

Étienne Balsan had been born into a wealthy family of fabric industrialists from Chatereoux; smart and innovative, the Balsan family had created a company which became extremely well-known for providing the army with uniforms. The Balsan name and company was a synonym of prestige during the Belle Époque era. It had been established in 1850 by Jean-Pierre Balsan, from the merger of the Manufacture de Drap du Park in Chateauroux with the Nerf mill factory on the Creuse river. Being a business pioneer, Jean had bought all the industrial equipment belonging to both factories.

The newly born Balsan factory was then redesigned and built by architect Henry Dauvergne and in 1860, the Balsan family moved to Chateauroux, to keep an eye on the business. The Balsans were not only innovators when it came to their work but also revolutionary when it came to their workers' wellbeing; they were the first to treat workers with respect by developing a social system which included education, healthcare and housing for their 800 employers.

The Balsan factory was also famous for creating the blue horizon cloth, a blue-grey cloth for the French army. Highly patriotic, the family had always shown their support to the army and in 1918, they officially were at the service of National Defence; to help the government, they started to make uniforms for soldiers.

On paper, Balsan would have been a perfect candidate for Coco, he was rich, smart, older and with a nose for fashion and business affairs, something that inspired Coco into becoming a businesswoman herself. When he met Coco, Balsan was a French socialite and heir, he played a pivotal role in the upper-class circle, but he was not an aristocrat or part of the landed gentry. He had two brothers, Robert and Jacques, who were both working in the family business and had married two women highly regarded by the society of the time, Aimée Seillière de Laborde, and Therese de Chabaud la Tour.

Jacques, later in his life, thanks to his connections, went on to marry Consuelo Vanderbilt, the former Duchess of Marlborough who also had a very interesting life. Described as slim, elegant and wealthy in her *New York Times* obituary in 1964, Consuelo Vanderbilt was the heiress of the Vanderbilt family fortune and the former wife of the Duke of Marlborough. She had never been in love with the duke as he had a reputation for being cold and snobby, and rumour has it that she had been forced to marry him by her mother, a challenging and difficult woman. Being a public figure, several New York papers of the time had published several features regarding her wedding, and some of them were satirical with a famous one portraying Consuelo as a bride kneeling next to the duke, her hands handcuffed behind her back and attached to a chain, held by her mother.

These stories of women and courtesans scented the air Coco was breathing at Compiègne, a cloud of inspiration which pushed her out of her shell as she started to connect with many high profile personalities of the time.

However, Balsan was never faithful to anyone, he loved women and had several extremely well-known lovers, one of them, maybe one of his most important ones was the French actress and courtesan Émilienne d'Alençon. The difference between a cocotte and a courtesan was fundamental at the time, a cocotte was a prostitute who also performed in low-key, third-class cafes while a courtesan, despite also being a prostitute, often came from a more artistic, educated background; they were attractive and used to accompany many influential men, often more than one at a time. Courtesans were wealthy and tended to be both free and dependent; free because they could never be conquered by just one man, and dependent because they relied on the men in their lives to fund their lifestyles.

In her conversations with Morand and other friends, Coco often spoke about her first years at Compiègne and how Étienne had kept many photographs of Émilienne in his house; she told Morand that she would have liked to have met her as she was so taken with her 'rival's' beauty, but that Balsan had, not surprisingly, been completely against the idea, at least at first. Rich and attractive, Émilienne d'Alençon was one of the best-known courtesans of the time and she developed advantageous relationships with some of the most important men in society, thanks to her beauty and photogenic face. Born in Paris, she had dropped her real name, Emilie André, after being advised by another courtesan that Émilienne would bring her more luck. Her powerful lovers would go to extreme measures. One was a duke called Jacques d'Uzès who fell madly in love with her and was so desperate to marry her that he was sent to Congo by his family in a desperate yet successful attempt to stop his infatuation. For quite some time, Émilienne was also the lover of the king of Belgium, Leopold II; the Prince of Wales future king Edward VII and of Kaiser Guillaume II. She was also rumoured to have had relationships with women, specifically with another courtesan Lian de Pougy who was both a lover and a rival. Later in her life, Lian married a Romanian prince while Émilienne became a writer, obtaining fame thanks to several poems including *Sous Le Masque*, one of her most popular ones. Much like other courtesans, Émilienne was part of the demimonde (in French, half world) a term coined by Alexandre Dumas in 1855 for the title of his play, which stood for a class of women of loose morals who played an important, active role in society.

Étienne was not thrilled by the idea of introducing Coco to his former lovers or friends; for him Mademoiselle Chanel was just another girl who he had taken in on a temporary basis, to be discarded once he was bored with her; a vision his wealthy, perhaps a little snobby friends must have shared. With some persistence, Coco did manage to meet Balsan's friends including Émilienne, and the two started an unlikely friendship as Émilienne was not jealous of Coco or any other of Balsan's lovers, and Coco, from her side, was way too much in awe of the gorgeous courtesan to feel like she could ever be a valid match to her beauty and charisma.

When seeing her beautiful pictures around Etienne's house, Coco must have felt the same frustration she had felt years before when comparing herself to the rich girls at Aubazine, that is probably why she started telling Etienne's friends about her romantic childhood and her nostalgic upbringing with her unpleasant but fair aunts to whom she owed everything. Coco also wanted to be loved, wanted by someone the way Balsan and several other men must have, she believed, wanted Émilienne.

Balsan was an officer in the cavalry and after leaving his career behind, he had started to breed horses and to participate in races. He was also an acclaimed polo player and owned the family-home in Chateau de Royallieu, a castle built on the ruins of the ancient Abbey of Royallieu, located in the heart of the Bayser fields. When he met Coco, he was clearly living the bachelor life surrounded by the things he loved the most: women and horses. And although moving to Compiègne had been Coco's choice, the choice of an adult woman taking life in her own hands and being responsible for that, she still felt she had been forced into a role she was not comfortable playing; during her *stay* at Chateau de Royallieu, Coco still felt she was being treated like a child.

It has never been clear how old Coco had actually been when she lived with Balsan. In her conversations with friends, she often said that she was younger than she really was; perhaps 16 years old. However, researchers have found that she was probably over 18. She told many of her friends that Balsan was not happy about the age gap, he was nervous about it and scared of being arrested by the police; and of the damage this would have done to his reputation. That was exactly why she was not allowed to write to anyone, no one could know that she was staying there with him, no one could know that she was his lover, or they could have told the authorities and he would have carried all the blame. However, for the society of the time, it was quite common for older men to start relationships with younger women who were often under the age of 18 and as Balsan had probably only been in his early twenties at the time, he was not much older than Coco.

Coco had followed Balsan to Compiègne, no one knew where she was, she was finally free but she felt that something was missing; she was often lonely as she was often forbidden from joining Balsan and his friends and was frequently left behind when they attended parties or events. She had not found a purpose, a goal to pursue, and she lacked the skills which would have helped her new social life; like piano playing or riding.

Coco felt very isolated and she was not able to write to family or friends, as that might have aroused suspicions of her whereabouts. Not one to do nothing, she threw all her energy into learning to ride. Later in her life, she would always remember how those moments on her horse, lost in the bucolic scenery of Compiègne, were her happiest times there.

Her time in Compiègne was not perfect, she found herself thrown into a society she didn't understand yet; a world of artists, socialites and affluent people who worked very little (and for pleasure) or not at all. Back in Moulins, she'd been doing three jobs and hadn't been around people who didn't work at all. Balsan was quite the playboy and not faithful to her; he had several other relationships whilst he was with Coco but that was part of the contract they had silently stipulated. During her time at the *chateau*, she spent her days horse riding, drinking coffee and reading novels in bed, something she particularly loved. It was also very important for Coco not to be like any other of Balsan's friends or lovers. Above all, she wanted to be herself, to speak her own mind and she didn't care if that embarrassed Balsan or any of his circle.

During her time in Compiègne, she did manage to make a few friends of her own and one of them was Gabrielle Dorziat who was a regular at the *chateau* and often came to visit Balsan with his good friend Léon de Laborde.

Dorziat was a French stage and film actress who had an extraordinary impact on Coco, she was the one to first go public with a Chanel creation, making the Chanel designs a must-have in any closet. Born in 1880, Gabrielle was extremely well- known for both her career and her romantic life, as she had been involved with some of the most popular actors of the time including Lucien Guitry and Louis Jouvet. Much like Coco, she also had entangled, powerful relationships with some of the strongest personalities of the time including Jean Cocteau, Jean Giraudoux, Paul Bourget and Henri Bernstein. In 1925, walking the same path many actresses of the time had walked before her, she married someone with a title, Count Michel de Zogheb, the cousin of King Fuad I of Egypt.

Coco and Gabrielle had a strong friendship despite Coco's inability to hide how charmed she was by the charismatic actress, especially in the beginning of their relationship. It was not unusual for Coco to have a contradictory relationship with women, especially with those she felt came from a more educated background than her. She did get along better with men and she could count on some of the most important men of the time as her friends. To her, women needed to be helped and supported all the time, something which she did not or could not, relate to; she felt she had very little in common with them and made no secret of that, as she often used to ridicule them, especially when she went to the races with Balsan where she would quite openly criticise the way those ladies dressed.

Coco was clearly not happy in Compiègne so she and Balsan decided to spend some time in Pau in the Aquitaine region, a beautiful setting standing between both the mountains and the ocean. There, she did not only hope to finally reconnect with Balsan who had grown more and more distant, making her feel like just another guest at the *chateau* but also to finally find a purpose in life, something she truly enjoyed.

At the *chateau* and with Balsan, she was still his kept woman and she could not help but feel trapped especially as she had no family support. By then, she didn't really have any relationship with her grandparents or aunts and even Adrienne had left her on her own. Adrienne, who was not only Coco's aunt but also her sister in everything but blood, had a different path to follow. After spending several years working as a seamstress with Coco and performing as a singer at little cafes in Moulins, she had fallen in love with Baron Maurice de Nexon and, despite his family being extremely against the idea of their son marrying a seamstress, they had made their union official in 1930.

Coco was left with endless, lonely days to fill; being a seamstress she started to show a stronger interest in fashion and out of boredom, began to make hats for Balsan's friends. The fashion style of the time was not something she was particularly fond of as it was too complicated and did not really enhance the female form; Coco believed that the fashion of the era had a way to hide women behind too many frills and feathers. It was not just about fashion, of course, fashion was intricately entangled into the politics of the time; the business of fashion was a complicated matter and to change it would have meant altering the status quo of French society.

During the Belle Epoque, fashion was often used as a way to express how affluent people were, that is exactly why women preferred elaborate garments and luxury, highly expensive fabrics. Not many could afford such fashion styles and fashion became a luxury only for a selected group, it was just another way of preserving the elite. Coco had very little if nothing in common with these people. She was not rich, she could not boast a family name of any importance and was, at the time, unemployed and staying at Balsan's as one of his several girlfriends; making her invisible to high society.

However, this did not stop her from expressing herself as she craved a simple yet more practical way to give voice to who she was and soon she dragged the rest of the, slightly reluctant, fashion world with her. It was no easy task as this was a time when women felt they had to show off what they owed and there was no room for subtlety. Fashion was much like today – it was exclusive, expensive and in its highest form, only really available to a few who would parade their latest outfits at intimate soirees and days out at the races. It was for the very best of French society to see, enjoy and to gossip about. Coco, who, sometimes, attended these events with Balsan, could not help but criticise the extraordinary number of feathers which were a must for hats and boas worn by the ladies of the time; she also loathed the puffiness of their skirts. Her background and family history had not made a fashionista out of her, but she had become someone, who despite everything, was a strict yet simple individual; she had been raised by nuns and her orphanage experience had somehow crept into her way of thinking, especially about fashion. To her, fashion should reflect those values of simplicity and practicality she had learnt how to endure at Aubazine, it was there that she had apprehended austerity as well as a more rigorous way of life; Aubazine was everywhere she looked and everywhere she made other women look when her designs and brand became an icon of style and elegance.

The year 1900 was a moment of confusion when it came to fashion, as Coco herself recalled during one of her conversations with Paul Morand: '1914 was still 1900, and 1900 was still the Second Empire, with its frenzy of easy money, its habits of straying from one style to another, of romantically taking its inspiration from every country and all periods, for it lacked a way of expressing itself honestly, and aesthetically pleasing appearance is never anything but the outer expression of moral honesty or authentic feelings.'

It was a confusing time for fashion and everything else, and with such a tumultuous vibe, fashion struggled to convey those values of honesty and authenticity.

Despite the luxury, the expensive clothes and the general confusion of the time, a little movement started to make itself known and available to the masses, which was essentially a crave and a desire for simplicity; the change was not immediate and fashion stayed excessive and elaborated for quite some time, much to Coco's disappointment; yet a subtle difference in style and garments became more visible. Women were still interested in making a statement, yet they started to appreciate the importance of being subtle.

Excess was still a favourite of the ladies of the time, but a more modest look started to make its way through. From puffy skirts to tailored clothes, the fashion word experienced a big change in its pace towards a simpler yet more elegant style. Coco Chanel did not only influence fashion, but she also gave a more contemporary definition; a new meaning of what being a lady meant. When suits for both men and women started to make an appearance, there was a public outcry as women wearing suits was seen as a defiance of power, of the patriarchal society, and for the first time, women took what could be seen as a visual step towards feminism.

Despite criticism, clothing became a little bit more practical. For the first time, different clothes had different purposes.

Women like Coco were expressing who they were and what they wanted even in fashion. Many people who could not afford the best that French couture could offer, still tried to emulate its designs with details in lace and delicate embroidery. Women were still wearing corsets to achieve a so-called great shape. Coco Chanel was one of the first designers to ban corsets from her creations.

Accessories were no less complicated. Hats, for example, seemed like a whole outfit on their own. Coco was never a fan of highly elaborated garments but absolutely detested Edwardian hats as she believed they hid women's faces and added very little, if anything, to their beauty. At that time, hats were a must-have accessory and again, they were highly intricate with their often-impractical addition of extra feathers and fabrics.

As Coco had predicted, the excesses of the Belle Époque were not going to last and especially after the war, more and more people started to take a stand against luxury, as it seemed inappropriate and a waste of money to spend so much on clothes when people's primary needs like food and water were lacking.

That is, exactly why, when it came to fashion, the difference between the nineteenth century and twentieth century was, for many, considered so huge. The war had changed people and there was no going back, money was scarce, and food represented a luxury only a few could afford; it was a time to be practical and many wished for a return to simplicity. It is no surprise then that such simplicity translated into a fashion style with fewer flowers and frills, both for men and women. People wanted to communicate a sense of austerity and a general awareness of how tough times had become. Chanel wanted to create new trends, something that included tailored suits and clothes based on comfort and practicality, she wanted women to be able to eat and move with ease without having to think about their corsets, and that is exactly what she did.

A lover of fashion and of the tailored look, Coco soon found the approval of Balsan's friends with her simple, tailored designs, something which still echoed of Aubazine: white and black, just like the nuns' white wimples and black skirts, became a recurring theme in Gabrielle's very own look and later in Chanel collections. At this stage in her life, fashion was still not her entire *raison d'être* yet and Balsan, despite being wealthy and well-connected, was not quite the man she was looking for; he had been generous and he would have been for many years to come yet she knew it wasn't right. She was also aware that she was not where she wanted to be yet; yes, she had made some changes already: dropped her name, borrowed another one from a song, she'd said goodbye to the ghosts of the past and abandoned her little girl's dreams. However, she felt something was missing in her life, something or maybe someone named Arthur Capel.

Chapter 4

Coco, the Woman

In 1924, Paul Morand, an actor, writer and good friend of Coco Chanel, published a novel, called *Lewis et Irène*. The story focuses on the romance between a French financial man Lewis and a young Greek widow Irène who meet after clashing over the acquisition of a sulphur mine in Sicily. Despite their differences and Lewis being an eclectic, adventurous type of guy, they fall in love and decide to settle down, embracing a domestic life. Their bucolic dream does not last long and soon boredom strikes; Lewis, who cannot cope with the *ennui* of leading a simple life, has an affair which drives Irène away. The couple breaks up whilst staying business partners.

Coco Chanel, a very good friend of Paul Morand, had a first edition of the book, which was in 2016 showcased during Culture Chanel, an exhibition focusing on Chanel and her extraordinary library. Her copy had a dedication from Morand himself saying: 'This Lewis who is a bit like Boy Capel [Arthur's nickname]'; it was a sweet dedication, Morand had based the character of Lewis on Boy Capel and in his dedication had not only admitted the connection but had also given a little comfort to his sweet friend Coco.

Coco and Morand had first met one uneventful night in 1909 and were introduced by an acquaintance they had in common, they had instantly liked each other and connected, the way many people of the time used to connect, at someone's house over drinks and endless chats about politics, the world and the arts.

The acquaintance in question was Misia Sert, a Polish patron, pianist and later a good friend of Coco herself. It all happened one night, back in 1921, as Morand remembered in his book *The Allure of Chanel*.

'I arrived at rue Cambon for the first time. A New Year's Eve party in 1921, I believe. "You are all invited to Coco's", Misia had said to us; all.'

Morand said that nothing in Coco that night would have suggested she was going to become the icon and the designer who went on to change the fashion world.

'You wouldn't have recognised Chanel's genius; there was nothing yet to suggest her authority, her violent rages, her belligerence, nothing that revealed that character destined for greatness.' Morand said that not even he would recognise in her the iconic woman whose name would, one day be on everyone's lips.

'Only Misia, with her commercial flair, had sensed that Chanel would ride to the top, had detected her serious side behind the frivolity, the precision of her mind and her talent, her uncompromising character,' wrote Morand.

Misia, after all, was half-envious, half fascinated by Coco and her smart, quick mind; in her 'incredible commercial flair', as Morand had put it quite so simply, Misia had once again, got past Coco's apparent shyness and deep pain for the loss of her beloved Boy Capel in a car crash, and had grasped Coco's essence, her genius. From his side, Morand said that Coco was so crushed by Capel's death that she had started questioning everything; that she must have thought that life would never be the same again.

'Behind an anxiety enlivened by so many guests, charming in her reticence, and of a shyness that was touching without one quite knowing why-perhaps because of her recent bereavement-Chanel appeared unsure of herself and as if she was questioning her life, no longer believing in happiness: we were bowled over. Did anyone suspect that we were dining, that evening, at the home of the exterminating angel of nineteenth-century style?' Morand remembered.

Morand was a French diplomat, novelist, playwright and poet; he also worked in politics serving as an ambassador in Bern. After graduating from the Paris Institute of Political Studies, he devoted his life to writing and worked on many short books. He was an anti-Semite and made no secret of that; according to French newspaper, *L'Express*, he would not let a day pass without criticising both Jews and homosexuals. Exactly like Coco, Morand liked to surround himself with some of the most influential intellectuals and artists of the time and was very good friends with Marcel Proust; and he loved nothing more than talking about him and was always particularly keen on recollecting the first time they had met. Morand met Proust one evening after a pleasant dinner with friends where the main topic had been Proust's À *La Recherche du Temps Perdu*. By reading Proust's latest remarkable work, he had found himself so captivated by the exquisite narrative and flowing words that he said that Proust's work was nothing short of a Flaubert. It had been Proust himself who had arranged a meeting with Morand; and in later interviews, Morand would always talk about the way Proust had been dressed that night; he had a long fur coat apparently, and Morand remembered that the rest of his clothes and his whole appearance seemed to have been frozen in 1905, the day he had decided to go to bed, only getting up from time to time and for special occasions.

Morand was an eclectic personality and being well-versed in the society of the time, he became an invaluable presence in Coco's life, especially when it came to documenting her memories as well as her most intimate thoughts. After the Second World War, Coco had invited Morand to visit her in Switzerland where she had a house, as she felt the need to share all her most secret thoughts; and she gave him the chance to write down all her best tales, her memories and impressions on the world and society; and she also gave him some precious insights into all the men in her life. Morand didn't do much with his notes until a year after Coco's death in 1971 when he decided to publish them as a memoir. In Morand's transcriptions of their long conversations, Coco gave some interesting yet sometimes fabricated anecdotes about the men in her life, her friends and her incredible journey through fashion and onto Chanel N°5. However, one of the most interesting passages is the one where Morand himself wrote about the night he had met Coco for the very first time, taking a perfect screenshot of what Coco was going through and how that night marked both the break with a dramatic, painful past and the beginning of a new phase in her life.

Coco, the icon, the fashion queen had been quite lonely and was in much need of new friends; she was grieving for her lover Arthur Capel and she felt lonely: 'Apart from her Deauville clients, or some polo players, friends of the Capel whom she had just lost, Chanel was very lonely, very shy, very closely watched; that evening Misia brought along people who would become Chanel's life-long companions, the Philippe Berthelots, Satie, Lifar, Auric, Segnonzac, Lipschitz, Braque, Luc-Albert, Moreau, Radiguet, Sert, Elise Jouhandeau, Picasso, Cocteau, Cendrars. Their presence alone marked the break with 1914, a past now dismissed, and a path that opened to the future...'

In his book, *Lewis et Irene*, Morand had been inspired by Arthur Capel and Coco's stories and her loving memories of him; in his narrative, he had crafted Lewis to be exactly like Arthur who had been Coco's most famous and important lover; from his physical description, black hair to his love for cars and horses, passions Capel also shared with Morand himself.

According to Lisa Chaney, biographer and author of *Coco Chanel: An Intimate Life*, *Lewis et Irene* marked the beginning of a different kind of literature, one in which women could be seen as strong characters who could function on their own both emotionally and financially; it was the first time that women started to be seen as powerful enough to carry a scene on their own; much like Coco, Irene was described as being a strong woman who despite falling in love, never forgot her goal in life and where she wanted to go. Heroines and the role of heroines were fundamental in Coco's life and stories, she had grown up reading romantic books and she still indulged into such novels from time to time; it was something that reminded her of her youth and gave her the comfort she needed when crushed under the weight of tragic events. At the time, Coco was still working on establishing her very own romantic narrative with Balsan, Capel and all her future lovers having an important influence on that.

Capel, far from being just another name to add to her long list of famous lovers, was her first and most important love; and much like any first love, he not only become some sort of idol to Coco, but he was, in fact, everything to Mademoiselle Chanel: her world, her life, and her motivation to go above and beyond in work. They had a challenging yet real relationship based on love, respect and pride, mostly Coco's pride; she wanted him to see her for who she really was, to be proud of her and to never be ashamed to introduce her to his friends; she had probably never felt anything like that before, it was the love story she would have crafted for herself if she could have, a love story about a young girl from Aubazine, nothing special on the surface yet someone who had managed to make this wonderful man fall deeply in love with her.

Capel was the love of her life and Coco, slowly distanced herself every day a little bit more from Balsan and from her role as a kept-woman; that was not the life for her – sure, she could have easily become a full-time courtesan but she decided against that. She was too proud and despite wishing for herself a lifestyle of wealth and luxuries, something that she had lacked all her life and something she definitely yearned for, she was not ready to compromise who she was and aimed to become financially independent only through her work.

Coco and Capel never married but Capel is believed to have proposed a few times; for the first years into their relationship, they were inseparable and spent all their free time together, but they never made their union official. Several pictures of the time illuminate their relationship; one, in particular, portrays both of them on the beach in Deauville, they sit close but hardly ever touch. Another interesting picture was taken when they were both in their twenties and at the very beginning of their relationship; in this particular picture, they almost kiss. The first time Coco and Capel met was in Pau where Balsan would often stay with friends, indulging in some of his favourite pastimes: playing polo and riding. Coco was, at the time, not very happy with her position as Balsan's lover as she felt she lacked both a purpose in her days as well as love itself.

Balsan was the man she had followed when escaping from a cheap destiny in Moulins yet he was not the man of her dreams, he could never be, they had hardly anything in common and she had a feeling he would have always looked at her the way a man looks at a kept woman, someone or even something that belongs to him. This didn't mean that they did not care for each other, Balsan had become very fond of Coco, and even decided to propose twice; maybe he was starting to see her more clearly or maybe he had finally realised her wit and talent but it was too late; Coco had already started looking for something else. She knew she wasn't cut for a life of luxuries she had not earned and as much as she loved spending her time riding Balsan's beautiful horses and reading her favourite books, she knew she had to focus on something else and assess her possibilities; maybe explore life itself a bit more, something that she couldn't have done had she decided to stay with Balsan.

Balsan did not want to lose Coco, his parents had died, and he could by then have easily married his lover without finding any real opposition to the relationship from his extended family or his influential friends. However, Coco was not the marrying type and dismissed Balsan's marriage proposals not once but twice.

She was planning her big move to Paris, and she made it clear that she was not in love with him and had no intention of getting married to him or anyone else; she wanted to work. She had been already very successful as a milliner for Balsan's friends and she wanted to open a hat shop in Paris; something Balsan was not thrilled about. What would people say? His lover, his courtesan, the woman he was supposed to support financially now had decided that she wanted to work. He expected the Parisian gossip to be insufferable, people would have said that he had not enough money to keep his woman happy; but Coco was decided. In order to give her what she wanted but also to save his reputation and keep an eye on her, Balsan offered Coco his Paris apartment in Boulevard Malesherbes for her to use as a fashion atelier.

It was not exactly what Coco had envisioned, and it was not the independence she had craved for. The Belle Époque was still bursting with prosperity and innovation, change was in the air and women were slowly yet effectively turning the status quo upside down; people wanted to play a role in such a change and to bring a little something of themselves into such a fascinating new time.

Much like Compiègne, in Pau, Balsan surrounded himself with the best of the bohemian, more artistic side of the French society, men of power, courtesans, actors, writers and socialites who would mingle and represent France and those fascinating times. He was not much interested in the aristocracy and in return, the aristocracy had not much interest in him; his friends often defied society's rules and for this, they were not extremely well-liked.

One of these friends, perhaps the one who did not exactly match his usual companions in their attitudes to rules and work was Capel. Capel was an Englishman who spoke perfect French and was often described as being self-made and independent from any family-inherited wealth; rather than being completely independent, he had chosen to work for a living despite not needing to do that yet he had not completely cut financial ties with his family. Born in Brighton, he was a polo player and the son of Arthur Joseph Capel, a shipping merchant; thanks to his mother Berthe André Lorin being French, he easily succeeded in engaging with the French society of the time and becoming one of its most sought-after personalities. He had certainly inherited a passion for ships from his father as well as his good looks, something that helped him his entire life. He had three sisters but no brothers and being the only son, he was required to attend several schools and to make a name of his own. According to biographer Lisa Chaney, Arthur Capel first attended Beaumont College, A Jesuit school at Old Windsor and then the college of Stonyhurst in Lancashire, one of the most important Catholic schools in the country. He received a strict, rigorous upbringing which was not too distant from the one Coco had endured at Aubazine.

The Beaumont College was a secular institution which dated back to 1861 and ran until its closure in 1967. It was managed by Jesuits, also called the Society of Jesus; this was a religious order of men affiliated to the Catholic Church and founded back in 1540 by St Ignatius of Loyola and a group of other people devoted to the Catholic principles. The Jesuits' influence was extending into the world as they were doctors, artists and astronomers. The Jesuits believed in seeking God and spirituality in every day's activity, doing the best they could with what they had at their disposal already and helping others.

This philosophy of life must have stricken a chord with Capel who was not only a businessman but also a spiritual soul devoted to improving his life and those of the people in his life. From a Jesuit school, Capel joined the Catholic college of Stonyhurst which already boasted a highly prestigious history by being one of Britain's most important boarding schools. By the time he arrived in Paris, he was something of a dandy.

During the Belle Époque, to be considered a dandy meant that you were a man who rejected bourgeois values and preferred to live a more relaxed life. Often, dandies were compared to bohemians, another group of men who rejected any aristocratic rules imposed by society. There was a slight difference between the two as bohemians were a little bit more concerned with values and principles rather than appearance and did not mind living in poverty to observe those values. Dandies were much more focused on their aesthetic and personal appearance; Charles Baudelaire, one of the most important and well-known dandies of his time, used to say that dandies had no other interest than grooming their very own appearance and elegance; they were those who aspired to everything that was sublime and beautiful in life. It goes without saying that leading such a dandy kind of life was a very expensive affair and this group of men usually came from the highest ranks of society. Much like Capel, dandies did not have royal blood but were still considered wealthy men who could afford such an extravagant lifestyle, spending part of their days focusing on and caring for their personal style and aesthetic. Such aesthetic reflected in the impeccable way dandies dressed from head to toe, paying particular attention to both fabrics and cuts. Dandies usually did not work as they did not have to, they tended to come from wealthy families and could easily live on their inheritances. Capel was different and he was one of the first to decide to work despite coming from a family of means.

Victor Hugo, another dandy of the time, was the one responsible for giving one of the most interesting and accurate descriptions when it came to dandyism; he said that a typical dandy could have been found gambling, smoking, drinking, and generally enjoying some very expensive pastimes which were often exclusive to the aristocracy. As mentioned before, these pastimes were very expensive, and many dandies couldn't afford to pay the bills; one of these was Baudelaire himself who lost everything he owned due to the dandyism lifestyle and he became a bohemian instead.

Capel never ran the risk of becoming a bohemian, he took different apprenticeships in his father's businesses in London, Paris and America and became closer to the aristocratic society of the time. He was not only an ambitious man but also someone who had found himself at the centre of some interesting rumours and would have done anything in his power to clear his name. Capel, who was often accused of keeping his family a mystery, much like Coco, hardly ever mentioned his parents, siblings or wealthy upbringing; for this reason, according to Chaney, he was often rumoured to be the illegitimate son of Jacob Emile Pereire, a banker from a Portuguese and Jewish background. To silence those rumours, and to make a name for himself, he started to work even harder than his father and surrounded himself with some of the most influential personalities of the time. Having Coco in his life represented a risk, she was not what he needed yet he had fallen in love with her and there was very little he could do about that.

Pau represented the perfect location for their first meeting; during their first encounter, despite not even talking that much, Coco found herself completely besotted with the Englishman. She knew the way she had known that Balsan would have been her easy escape from a little life in Moulins that Capel would be the love of her life, it was love at first sight for both of them. Capel was not a close friend of Balsan's, they had been acquainted for quite some time, yet their relationship had remained superficial. He could not bring himself to stay far away from Coco and her new boutique, Balsan's boutique, in Boulevard Malesherbes. Their relationship was new and exciting and something Coco had never experienced in her life before; jealous and afraid to lose his lover, Balsan proposed to Coco again but Coco refused him; she now only had eyes for Capel.

At first, Coco maintained a relationship with both Balsan and Capel, without making a mystery of her preference for the dandy Brit, but it was pretty clear that she was in love with Capel, yet she could not help but care for Balsan as well. She was grateful for everything he had done for her, for giving her a life she could have only dreamt of. It was not just about being grateful to her old friend and lover, Coco was a smart woman and she must have recognised that Balsan was someone influential within French society; and having him as an enemy would have certainly not done her, Capel, or, let alone, her upcoming business venture any favours.

Yet, she could perceive the difference between the two men in her life and she could also sense who she became in the presence of one or the other. Balsan was a friend, someone who had given her the very first taste of the life she was destined to have, while Capel was, quite simply, the love of her life. Coco had never experienced anything like that before. She couldn't help herself, she left Pau the day after, with the absolute certainty that once in Paris, she would have followed Capel everywhere he went. Slowly, without arousing any suspicious in Balsan, or at least not that many, she made a few adjustments to her life; she left Chateau de Royallieu and moved to a suite at The Ritz Hotel in Paris, something Capel had insisted on, she also spent quite some time at Capel's apartment at Le Champs-Élysées, sharing a flat and unofficially becoming his new girlfriend.

With Capel, she shared a strong relationship, intimate yet fiercely independent; she accepted his money but once financially more stable and with her affairs going well, and with the boutiques making profits, she returned everything she had borrowed and made her business stand on its own. After a while, Balsan let his pride go and invited the new couple back to the Chateau de Royallieu; he had other lovers, other businesses to attend to, and so he ended up leaving Coco to enjoy her new relationship. Balsan and Coco stayed friends for the rest of their lives; he was a strong presence in Coco's life, first offering his very own studio in Boulevard Malesherbes and then financially supporting her in her business venture. Coco went on to open several boutiques, including one in Deauville, a fashionable and beautiful city. Deauville was a resort designed by architect Desle-François Breney who had been inspired by Baron Haussmann's redevelopment of Paris. Within just a few years, the resort had boomed and was now boasting some of the most interesting characters of the time as its celebrity guests.

Both Balsan and Capel, would send their most affluent lady friends to Coco's Deauville shop and urge them to buy her latest creations, having an extraordinary impact on her business.

Capel supported Coco as a woman and a designer, he was the only man in Coco's life, and she would have married him had she not been so fiercely independent and single-minded. Capel was the one to believe in Coco and her talent first as a milliner and as a businesswoman, he was the one to finance Chanel's career and very first boutiques. Capel was an eclectic personality, often described as an intellectual; he was a strong sponsor of the Chanel designs and not only financially supported Coco and her boutique but also served as an inspiration for her designs. Many believe that it is thanks to Capel that Chanel started to explore the boy look after beginning to steal some of his tweed jackets to wear herself. He had, after all, an exquisite fashion sense which deeply affected Coco and her very own designs and he provided Coco with endless inspiration which culminated in the creation of the Boy jersey which added a masculine, innovative touch to her designs. By the time he met Coco, Capel was already a wealthy man with influential friends who had charisma, generosity and could hardly refuse Coco anything.

Capel was different from Balsan. If Balsan had a more relaxed approach to the rules imposed by the society of the time and often made his own, along the way; Capel was not going to play against the rules, as he always felt he could not; his ambition was too strong and this was one of the things he shared with Coco, they were both so ambitious they would stop at nothing in order to reach their goals.

Capel had some powerful connections in the highest ranks of French society and because of his businesses, he was, after all, a self-made, man who worked for a living, he could not afford to fall in love with anyone. Despite adoring Coco and having turned their affair into a somewhat stable relationship, he was not that flexible when it came to introducing

Coco to some of his friends from the French aristocracy. It was nothing new for Coco as she had experienced something similar with Balsan at the beginning of their relationship; yet if Balsan's friends were mostly dandies and artists who engaged into risky relationships with actresses and courtesans, Capel's circle came from a higher level and would not have been happy to accept her and her background.

Coco was not happy about it, she loved the man and would have done anything for him; but being treated like that went against her pride and no one had more pride than Coco, not even Capel. Once, in order to make her presence known and accepted by Capel's elitist world, Coco managed to persuade Capel into attending an important gala in Deauville together as a couple; there, she not only managed to charm the exclusive high society of the time but also marked her territory as Arthur Capel's new girlfriend. Once again, she had done something a romantic heroine from one of her books would have done, despite knowing her place and not wanting to upset Capel, she had made the rational decision to step out of the darkness and to tell the world, in this case, the snobby society of the time, about who she was and who she was with.

Thanks to Capel, his connections and his financial help, she successfully opened rue Cambon in 1909, with her apartment sitting at the top of the Chanel boutique and salon. The apartment and the boutique were connected by a curved staircase in beige where Coco used to sit and discreetly watch the audience so she could gauge their reaction to her collection. The street where her boutique was located, rue Cambon was a vibrant place which took its name after a famous rebel elected to the National Convention in the eighteenth century, Pierre-Joseph Cambon. Much like Pierre, rue Cambon was a street of change and innovation with new buildings affected by different styles including classicism which stood out for the simplicity of line, rigour and a sense of smoothness. Coco opened Chanel Modes, her hat shop, at Number 21 Rue Carbon in one of the most fashionable parts of Paris which soon became a focal point for artists and personalities of the time. It was also popular with writers like Stendhal and Chateaubriand as well as for caricaturist George Goursat known as SEM who created the first artistic caricature of Chanel N°5.

In 1918, Coco bought the entire building at Number 31 and launched a modern boutique; an innovative concept for the time. By 1921, she was not only displaying her fashion accessories, including her beautiful hats there, but also her very first perfume, N°5. Later, she also added jewellery and beauty products inspired by her childhood at Aubazine. Gaining more and more encouragement from her customers, she expanded even further and by 1927, Coco occupied five buildings on rue Cambon. The rue Cambon original boutique was on the ground floor with the large reception on the first floor being used to introduce her collection to the world as well as for fittings for her haute couture dresses creations. The second-floor apartment was a private studio where she often spent time alone thinking about her new collection or just reading her favourite books.

Those were the years where Coco really established herself as a businesswoman, she was happy, finally she had found that purpose she had been looking for ever since her times at Aubazine; she was not an orphan anymore but a woman who had managed to take destiny into her own hands and had become someone she could be proud of, and indeed, Capel could admire.

Coco and Capel were lovers and business partners as well, he became the most important person in Coco's life, inspiring her life and her art. Talking later about her jersey garments, she said that the idea had come after a particularly cold day in Deauville, a place which was very dear to her and Capel. In 1919, after Capel's tragic death, Coco started to wear black dresses to mark her grief and claimed the whole world would have worn black with her: the little black dress was born.

Coco and Capel had a complicated relationship, despite their love, they would not ever fully belong to each other. Coco was proud of her independence, after all, she had reimbursed him fully and was going to be a woman who could support herself. Capel, who was equally proud, was looking for a woman from a more aristocratic background. Deauville became the favourite location of their romantic liaison where

Coco opened a second boutique in Gontaut-Biron which proved to be even more profitable than the one on rue Cambon for its exclusive, selected clientele.

The year 1914 marked the end of the Belle Époque and the beginning of The First World War which lasted until 1918 and involved most of the nations in Europe as well as Russia, The United States, the Middle East and other regions. The war saw Germany, Austria-Hungary and Turkey fight against France, Russia, Italy, Great Britain and later, the United States. Capel told Coco to move to Deauville and to keep the boutique open; with most hotels, including their favourite The Royal, where they had stayed several times, being turned into hospitals, French people were in no mood for luxury but Coco's creations were something else, and her boutique managed to stay open for a large part of the war. She was after all the creator of the *pauvre genre*. According to *Time*, Chanel invented the so-called 'poor look' by putting women into men's jersey sweaters and creating simple dresses based on sailor tricot; she also used a mechanic's blouse, a waitress' white collar, cotton dresses and shoes with no back. *Time* also went on to praise the designer for the simplicity of her clothes and the use of ordinary fabrics; her luxury designs were in Coco's own word the very opposite of vulgarity.

Paris was not safe anymore and most French people had either moved to Bordeaux as urged by Marshal Joseph Jacques Césaire Joffre who was in charge of the military operations during the First World War. Capel was first commissioned as a second lieutenant in the Cavalry division and then enlisted and joined the British Expeditionary Forces, the home-based British army forces that supported the left of the French armies during the First World War. This force was formed as a consequence of the army reform in 1908 and sponsored by Richard Burdon. Before the reform, it was common practice to dispatch units as individuals and organise them into larger units once they were on location. However, in the twentieth century, it became apparent that it would have been more efficient for units of the British army to be trained as units before the beginning of any war.

Capel also joined an intelligence unit under George de Symons Barrow who came from a military family and was the son of a major-general in the Indian army. He joined Coco first in Deauville and then in Biarritz several times where he urged Coco to open another boutique. In the meantime, Coco who was living a personal drama with her sister Julia's sudden death, had decided to adopt André Palasse, Julia's child and together with Capel, had made the choice of sending the boy to Beaumont, Capel's old boarding school, where the boy would have received a Catholic education.

The Biarritz resort had been a favourite beach getaway since Napoléon III and his Spanish-born wife Eugénie, the glitz and glam were the perfect way for French people to take their mind off the brutality of the First World War.

Coco's sister, Antoinette, who had already helped her with the opening of the Deauville boutique also went to support Coco with the new shop in Biarritz, which boasted some of Coco's friends including opera singer Martha Davelli and socialite Kitty Rothschild as some of its most prestigious clients; however, most of Coco's clientele came to the Biarritz boutique from across the border from Spain.

What was anticipated as a quick war lasted four years and involved the rest of the world, France included. Much like her fellow French people, Coco and her friends, refused to believe the war would have lasted any longer than a couple of years and were not particularly concerned about that changing their lifestyle. They were wrong, after the war, both Coco and Capel would have changed their attitude and approach towards society and most importantly, towards each other.

Despite the victory, the war had lost France precious lives and resources, with at least 1.3 million men killed and about 1 million left with disabilities. With a large part of France's most prosperous agricultural areas being completely devastated, there was very little to live on for those who had been lucky enough to survive the war. Things were not any better from an industrial point of view with the national production falling to 60 per cent compared to more prosperous years before the war. The general morale was nothing like the lights and the sparkle of the Belle Époque when an innovative, positive spirit had infected society and its people; there was no more time to waste at cafes, drinking, dancing and enjoying time with cocottes or just talking about the world and the arts endlessly; courtesans, as well, were now a thing of the past and so was a more frivolous approach to fashion. Coco had predicted it all and by already favouring practicality over flowers, feathers and frivolity, she had a distinct advantage over other fashion designers.

From his side, Capel had become even wealthier as his coal business had become more profitable. He decided to venture into the political world and started looking for a wife who would be a better social fit than Coco. Despite being in love with Coco, he married Diana Wyndham and had two daughters; the reason behind his marriage to a British society lady was never fully explained. Desperate with jealousy, Coco believed that he needed a better-educated woman from British high society, something she could never ever be. Yet, many biographers believe that Capel had proposed to Coco first, but that Coco had not been ready for marriage. In many ways, Diana was a perfect candidate, much more appropriate than Coco. Born in Ascot, Diana had been married before to Percy Wyndham, who was killed in First World War. She was a trained nurse and would tend to the wounded during the war; she was a perfect match for Capel.

Diana represented everything Capel had wanted from society, she was an aristocratic, well-known, educated woman who had served in the First World War; someone to take to social events, someone who would have been approved of and who could add solidity to his already well-established public persona. Coco couldn't have taken Capel's decision to marry someone else lightly, and letters found by Chaney seemed to suggest that far from marrying Diana over Coco because of her social superiority, he instead felt intimidated by Coco and her single-mindedness. After all, Coco had reimbursed the money Capel had lent her for her business and she was becoming more and more confident and independent. She had opened three different boutiques in France and during a challenging time, and Coco's confidence and new-found strength started to scare Capel and make him insecure. He recognised Coco's personality, business mind and talent but he was also taken by Diana's femininity and predictability. He had had different affairs with several women but had never left Coco, he was in love with her, and yet he recognised that in order to excel both from a business point of view and in politics, he had to let her go and embrace Diana.

Coco and Capel never stopped being lovers, it was impossible for both of them to give up on each other, many believe that his marriage with Diana was already over by the time of Capel's car crash in 1919 but Coco knew better. Diana was three months pregnant with his second child.

Chapter 5

Coco, the Designer

From fashion weeks to adverts, movies, books and documentaries, Chanel is familiar, but it is exclusive, it is luxury and yet it is personal too. It is the feeling we assume that people – artists belonging to Coco's circle must have felt when spending time with her, in rue Cambon, lounging on her sofa, conversing about the world, breathing in her iconic Chanel N°5 essence. Far from being just an accessory and then a fashion designer, Coco was a visionary, an artist in her own right, and someone who could put a successful, positive spin on anything she did in her life.

In one of her conversations with Morand, she said about her role as a designer: 'I was working towards a new society. Up until then, they had been clothes designed for women who were useless and idle, women whose lady's maids had to pass them their stockings; I now had customers who were busy women; a busy woman.'

As we all know already, Coco started as a milliner, with her shop in rue Cambon soon becoming a pivotal place where women from both high society and more artistic, bohemian circles would gather to buy Mademoiselle's latest collections. She was not the only dressmaker making a name for herself in Paris of course, she was living in a time where she would be inspired by fellow milliners and designers. One of these was another French designer, Jeanne Lanvin, who like Coco had started out as a milliner before moving into dressmaking.

Jeanne was a haute couture designer who founded both the Lanvin fashion house and the perfume company with the same name. Born in 1867, she was about 20 years older than Coco and she was a Parisian girl who exactly like Coco had had to work hard for her success. She was the eldest of the eleven children of Constantin Lanvin and Sophie

Deshayes and at the age of 16, she became an apprentice milliner for Madame Félix in Paris and trained with milliner Suzanne Talbot before becoming a milliner herself on the rue du Faubourg Saint-Honoré in 1889.

At this time, the style of these particular hats left very little to the imagination and were nothing like Coco's; they were bigger and more pompous, and they sat on elaborated structures and were usually finished with extravagant decorations which also included soft feathers and flowers. A newspaper article by *The New York Times* in 1914 reported that Talbot also used lacquered daisies and dahlias, apparently her favourite flowers, for her hats. It was all a far cry from Coco's style who would always strive for simplicity and elegance; something easily mistaken for austerity.

Jeanne, a savvy business woman herself, decided to expand her business further and with Coco being busy with her hats and not much of competition in Paris, she decided, in 1909, to start designing and making high couture dresses; this is when she joined the Syndicat de la Couture and officially became a couturier. As it often happens, chance played its role and as Jeanne started to make dresses for her daughter Marguerite, whom she adored, more and more mothers started to request similar dresses for their own daughters; from daughters to mothers, the step was short, too short in fact, and almost immediately, Jeanne started to work on dresses for women and to sell them in Europe and her Paris boutique on the rue du Faubourg Saint-Honoré started to become popular with the wealthy Parisian women of the time.

Coco must have looked at Jeanne with deep admiration and found in her the inspiration she needed to expand her own business from hats to dresses.

The fashion house of Lanvin not only expanded to include a dye factory in Nanterre but also went above and beyond that, and she succeeded in launching different shops which sold dresses and also specialised in home decor, menswear, furs and lingerie. Much like Coco, Jeanne also created a signature fragrance called Arpège which was inspired by Jeanne's young daughter and the sound she made while practising her scales on the piano. Jeanne, who loved to be in the company of artists and influential people of her time, started in 1922, several, highly successful collaborations with French designer Armand-Albert Rateau; they worked together on the full redesign of her homes and boutiques. It is difficult to understand whether Jeanne Lanvin ever felt that she was in competition with Coco; but one thing is certain, they had several things in common including a passion for interiors. Coco, in fact, not only had an exceptional taste in fashion but also in home décor, and she made both her boutiques and her suite at the Ritz stand out because of their iconic interiors.

Jeanne went on to develop a strong relationship with Armand-Albert Rateau, a famous interior designer, who designed for her some remarkable bronze furniture and not only become Lanvin's manager of Lanvin-Sport but was also responsible for designing the Lanvin perfume flacon for Arpège. Rateau also helped Jeanne to manage Lanvin-Décoration, an interior-design department, established in 1920 in the main store on the rue du Faubourg Saint-Honoré. Jeanne's relationship with Rateau was like Coco's with Capel – a very successful partnership. The similarities did not end here and just like Coco, her childhood had inspired her famous, iconic trademark, Jeanne's Arpège perfume containers were also inspired by young Marguerite and are still today decorated with Paul Iribe's gold image of Jeanne with Marguerite. Lanvin was also another romantic heroine of her time, as romance seemed to inspire these women and their art, and she married twice: the first time to Count Emilio di Pietro, an Italian nobleman, Marguerite's father, and later to journalist and later French consul Xavier Melet.

With Jeanne focusing more on dressmaking, a spot in the millinery world in Paris made itself open and Coco decided that it was a good time to make her debut with her designs.

Thanks to Balsan and Capel's powerful friends and her innate business flair, Coco quickly gained popularity and her hats found the approval of several local and national magazines with enthusiastic reviews and pictures of Coco modelling her own hats starting to invade Paris and the rest of France. After all, hats were the accessory of the time, as any woman would feel naked without the appropriate headwear; it was also the norm to see women wearing hats inside often at the theatre and the opera.

Women had as many hats as they had dresses, for different occasions and outfits, it was as important as grabbing a jacket and it defined your social status. Coco's hats had nothing in common with those of the past, she was focused on making chapeaux for women, to celebrate their beauty, not to hide their features.

Deauville became an important milestone location for Coco. It was there that she started to expand her collections, slowly moving from hats to beach accessories, the little beach resort offered her the perfect location and clientele for a new fashion collection. While spending more and more time in Deauville with Capel, she paid attention to the people who would populate its glamorous beaches and decided to specialise in comfortable beachwear and sportswear which for the time proved to be quite a novelty; at the time, women were not used to wearing beachwear and mostly used to fully dress when going to the beach. In Deauville, Coco sold blouses which were worn over soft skirts, lightweight shoes and canvas suits; in her new boutique, she was not on her own and she was helped by her aunt and friend Adrienne, who being just as gorgeous as Coco, managed to attract the attention of everyone in Deauville turning the boutique into a very popular spot.

Even when the First World War broke out, Coco, who had not returned to Paris and stayed in Deauville under Capel's advice, managed to dress not only the nurses staying at the hospital but also the wealthy beachside clientele who were bored of the war and looking to add something new to their wardrobes; she even arrived to cut jersey from sweaters when it became challenging to source new fabrics.

She was not only a designer, she was also an artist who loved to work with other artists and that is probably why later in her life, she turned her attention to the world of the arts. She had made such a name for herself in the fashion world that artists started to ask for her support on different projects including costume designs for the ballet. Her designs were anything but classic and she was known as someone who would

Coco Chanel: A New Portrait by Marion Pike (2013), Fashion Space Gallery, London College of Fashion UAL, Exhibition installation photographs by Daniel Caulfield-Sriklad.

FASHION SPACE GALLERY

COCO CHANEL: A NEW PORTRAIT
BY MARION PIKE, PARIS 1967-1971

The Exhibition: Evolution & Interpretation

Jeffie Pike Durham contacted me after reading my monograph Chanel Couture and Industry (V&A, 2011). I had referenced a 1969 photo shoot by David Bailey for American vogue. The models, dressed by Chanel, posed before two huge portraits of Coco, painted by Marion Pike.

Jeffie showed me her extraordinary Archive, which she contextualised with poignant spoken memories. Objects and narrative, two core elements of curatorial practice, combined to form the basis of a fascinating exhibition. Curatorship excites the aesthetic and intellectual interpretation of objects to construct meanings. A comparison between Marion and Coco's life stories suggested numerous similarities and binary opposites. And, various themes emerged.

The artisanal name (with its five digits) and the eyes form prominent motifs. Like biography, portraiture seeks to capture the likeness and unique essence of a character. Coco was known for the penetrating intensity of her eyes. In self portraits Marion's own gaze is direct and lacks guile. Marion and Coco enjoyed five years of friendship. Jeffie owns five paintings of Coco and Chanel's lucky number was five.

As Marion travelled extensively, the processes of packing/unpacking clothing influenced the photographic styling and display of exhibited garments. Creating an exhibition is a team endeavor (see Credits). LCF graphic designer David Harris drew references from the typography, layout and materiality of late 1960s fine art books. Simon Jones, the exhibition designer, provided inspired solutions that are sensitive to objects and narrative, with flexibility for touring.

Amy de la Haye, Curator
Professor, Rootstein Hopkins Chair of Dress History & Curatorship,
Joint Course Leader, with Judith Clark, for the MA Fashion Curation pathway
London College of Fashion

Coco & Marion

Marion and Coco were introduced via Frederick Brisson, a mutual friend who produced the Broadway musical 'Coco' (1969). The first time Marion went to her salon, Coco kept her waiting and so she sketched what she saw around her. Chanel could be highly critical and aloof. When she viewed Marion's drawings she credited her as 'a real artist'. She then removed her own scarf and placed it around Marion's neck, to mark the beginning of their friendship.

The women experienced very different life stories. Marion's biography was privileged and nurturing, whilst Coco's childhood was impoverished and lacked love. Both of their mothers died when they were children and they each experienced the suicide of a close family member. As women, they challenged gender norms by living independent lives, dedicated to their chosen métier. Both adored the opera, horse riding and appreciated the functionality of menswear clothing styles.

Coco romanticised her past and destroyed personal documents before she died. Conversely, Marion left masses of evidence and never 'managed' her biography. It is the items Marion chose to preserve that are exhibited.

A snapshot, taken at Chanel's house in Lausanne, captures Marion and Coco laughing together: their mutual affection is tangible. Neither woman retired – the final days of each life were fulfilled by work. When she heard that Chanel had died, Marion was painting sublime skyscapes in Barbados...

Louise de Vilmorin (1902-69)

Louise de Vilmorin was an author, poet and society hostess. One of her best-known novels is Madame de (1951). It is an object-centred tale about a pair of diamond earrings that move in and out of the protagonist's life.
Chanel met Louise in Venice in 1947 and invited her to write her autobiography.
Unable to substantiate the stories that Chanel told her, the writer despaired. In 1948, Chanel brought the project to a halt. She could not entrust her life story to another.
Marion met Louise in 1960 and painted two portraits of her (1961 and 1966). The art theorist André Malraux was Louise's partner. Marion thought he was the most fascinating man she ever met. It was Malraux who stated that, 'The art museum is one of the places that give us the highest idea of man.'

Rosalind Russell (1908-76)

Rosalind 'Roz' Russell was a leading Hollywood actress, who was cast as an elegante, and in comedic roles. Fellow actor Cary Grant introduced her to the musical producer Frederick 'Freddie' Brisson, whom she married in 1941.

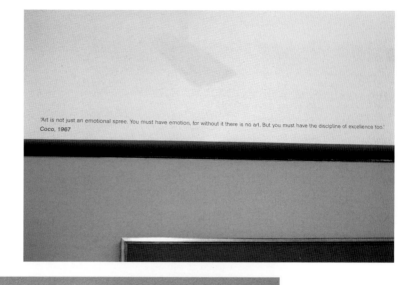

'Art is not just an emotional spree. You must have emotion, for without it there is no art. But you must have the discipline of excellence too.'
Coco, 1967

Chanel (1883-1971)

'A dress is neither a tragedy, nor a painting; it is a charming and ephemeral creation, not an everlasting work of art.' Chanel

In 1967 Chanel was 84 years old, her hands ravaged by arthritis. She continued to work six days a week. In October 1967 she presented her spring/summer 1968 collection. She hung Marion's recently completed 'Coco Chanel: Big Head' and 'Chanel in her Atelier' prominently at her catwalk show.

Chanel presented comfortable, elegant, understated – but never unremarkable – softly tailored suits and stylish dresses. To these she added more trend-led designs, such as the brocaded silk lamé tailored shorts ensemble made for Marion. Exquisite materiality and meticulous craftsmanship were hallmarks of her luxurious haute couture garments. She also made everyday working trousers for Marion.

Out of the public eye, Coco could be affectionate and comedic: it was this "side" of her that so enchanted Marion and Jeffie.

Chanel was superstitious. Her lucky number was 5 and she adored lions, the motif of her August birth sign. The luxurious, sheepskin-lined, wool coat she gave Jeffie features her signature metal buttons with domed lion heads. She was buried in Lausanne: her tombstone features five carved lion heads.

'Chanel Seated', 1968
Acrylic on masonite board
107 x 118cm

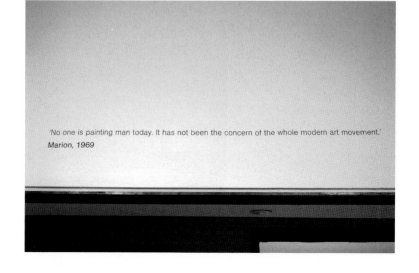

'No one is painting man today. It has not been the concern of the whole modern art movement.'
Marion, 1969

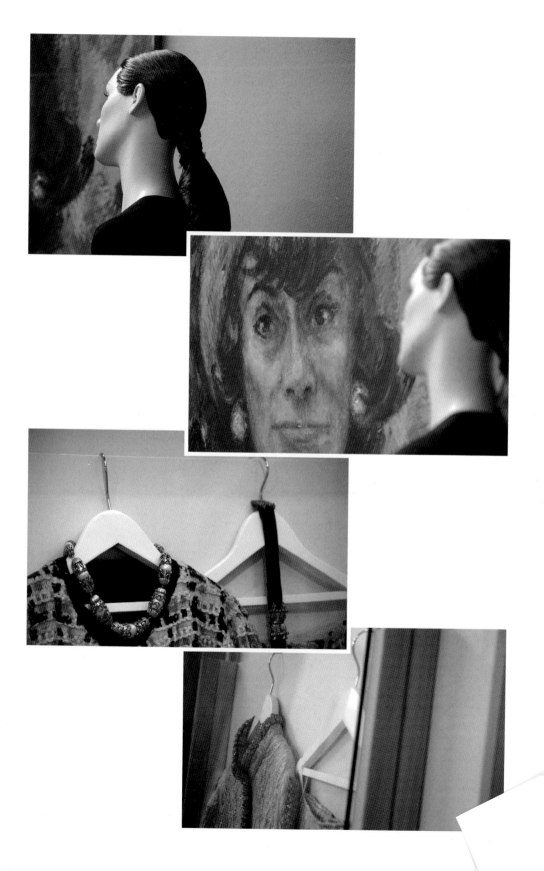

'Pont Neuf in Winter', 1971
Acrylic on masonite board
107 x 90cm

'Paris Rooftops', 1971
Acrylic on masonite board
136 x 125cm

'Pont Neuf at Night', 1971
Acrylic on masonite board
125 x 137cm

A stamp printed in Republic of Guinea commemorating Coco Chanel. (*By neftali*)

Portrait of Coco Chanel. (*By Vegan Girl*)

Chanel shop in old Marais quarter. (*By Elena Dijour*)

Chanel on the lamppost in Westminster city borough. (*By Phaustov*)

Gabrielle Chanel Coco portrait illustration. (*By Natata*)

Karl Lagerfeld and Virginie Viard walk the runway after the Chanel show. (*By FashionStock.com*)

Paris: Models walk the runway finale during the Chanel show. (*By FashionStock.com*)

New York, 2018: A billboard depicting a sketch of Coco Chanel. (*By Daniel J. Macy*)

Gabrielle (Coco) Chanel (1883–1971), iconic French fashion designer, pictured by her car in fashionable Biarritz.

A camera study of Gabrielle Bonheur, Coco Chanel (1883–1971).

Marion Pike
painting on the
Pont des Arts in
Paris, 1968

Marion Pike painting Rembrandt at the Louvre, 1958

defy fashion rules as well as for being a rebel; for this reason, she managed to attract the attention of Sergei Diaghilev, Russian art critic, patron and founder of ballet company Ballet Russes. Coco not only started to work with him but also joined him and his friends of artists becoming a patron to them all. Many designers and artists of the time started to work for the Ballet Russes including Pablo Picasso; it was during her time supporting the company that Coco came in contact with a young dancer, Alicia Markova; the pair would often meet while Coco offered her expertise during Sergei's costume rehearsals. Alicia was one of Sergei's favourites and soon became his first ballerina, choreographer, director and teacher of classical ballet.

The Ballet Russes always had a way to stand out for its one of a kind costumes as well as its outstanding music and choreography. As a born rebel, Coco was the perfect creative partner as she was not scared to express herself in fashion, no matter how irreverent her ideas and designs could seem. She started to receive worldwide recognition and many artists began to reproduce her designs in their works. One of these was Pablo Picasso; Coco was the one whose bathing suits were painted by Picasso in his work *Women Bathing* dated 1918; her bathing suits had the merit of marking the start of a new fashion era; with these new, innovative, often considered scandalous, creations being skirtless and sleeveless: an outrageous change for the time.

Coco also began to design sports clothes and that pushed Diaghilev to ask her to work on his new production Le Train Bleu; *le train* was based on the real train which would bring wealthy people to Monte Carlo. Written by another good friend of Coco's, Jean Cocteau, the production had the choreography by Bronislava Nijinska. It was a satire, a critique, which made fun of the wealthy French people who used to spend their summer and money in Monte Carlo. Coco was an exceptional fit for *le train*, she did not lack humour and years before, whilst Balsan's lover, she had been the one to poke fun at the wealthy women going to the races in Compiègne for their unnecessary, elaborated, outfits. Diaghilev wanted Coco to embody some of her original and controversial style into the costumes for his dancers, this resulted in several polemics, not much from the audience as much as from the dancers themselves, who felt as if they would go almost naked on stage. Lydia Sokolova was forced to dance on stage with a bathing costume in wool jersey and slippers while also wearing big pearls earrings, Coco's distinctive jewellery trademark, which were so big she could hardly hear the music. Despite this, the audience loved Coco and her new, refreshing attitude to fashion; she was a designer like no one else. They were mesmerised by the story of *le train* as well as by Mademoiselle's fashion style.

Coco was becoming an icon, someone who would inspire many as a designer and an artist among other artists, with several of these becoming some of her closest friends and lovers.

Chapter 6

Coco, the Lover

We know by now that Coco Chanel was many things and yet much like many women before or after her, she established a reputation, good or bad, for the men in her life. Her name was always everywhere, gossip chased her wherever she went, and it did not help that she could always be found with some of the most interesting personalities of the twentieth century. She was fortunate enough to establish connections with several high-profile men, often acting as their patron or by being in business with them. It wasn't just about Balsan or Capel either, as in her lifetime, she fell in love several times and with some of the most well-known names of the 20th century.

Coco and Stravinsky

Many researchers and writers have tried to understand the relationship between Coco and Russian musician Igor Stravinsky. It was a love, a passion, an affair; nothing like Coco had experienced before, a bond she had not been ready for, a connection completely different to the ones she had with previous lovers. Capel has always been labelled as Coco's one true love but if Capel was the love of her life, the one who had given shape and meaning to her younger years, Stravinsky was the consuming passion she experienced when she was a little older and had already become a fashion icon. If with Balsan and Capel, she had always felt a little insecure, with Stravinsky, she finally felt like an active part of a relationship, a more adult partnership which saw her being, maybe for the first time, at a distinct advantage.

They met for the first time when Coco attended the premiere of *Rite of Spring* in 1913. Later the musician lost everything during the

Russian Revolution and he, his wife and four children went to live with the designer. Coco had taken an interest in his misfortunes and, much like her good friend Misia Sert, acted as a patron to the Stravinsky family. Being independent and rich certainly helped her position, Coco was in a very positive place financially as she had opened boutiques in Deauville and Biarritz as well as Paris during the Second World War and was finally starting to see the profits of all her hard work.

According to different sources, the affair only lasted a few months but still today, it is remembered as being a very important moment in both their lives. Some biographers claim that the affair lasted longer and that it continued for several years after; with the couple influencing each other artistically as Coco created the iconic Chanel No.5 and Stravinsky made his powerful music transition from modernism to neo-classicism. It is claimed that Coco liberated Stravinsky sexually with this resulting in his music finding the inspiration it needed. Misia, Coco's overbearing, overprotective friend, was not happy about the affair; it was difficult to understand if she had a genuine interest in Coco and wanted to protect her or if she was purely jealous of Coco who was becoming not only more and more independent from her but also starting to have her own, vital position as part of the French society. After the grief for her poor Capel, Coco had turned herself from inexperienced, broken-hearted designer to a successful businesswoman; she was a socialite, a patron and an important figure for French artists, something Misia could not help but feeling jealous of. Also, it was quite prestigious for Coco to have such an important personality in her home, as sometimes she still felt like the orphan from Aubazine and having such an inspiring musician as her guest was incredibly important for her, her business and her public persona.

A jealous and potentially concerned Misia tried to persuade Stravinsky to leave Coco alone and to think about his wife, something which he eventually did; Coco did not like Misia interfering in her affairs, she was grateful to her for being a close friend while in mourning for Capel but she felt better now; she was an independent woman whose fame and financial stability had given her a much stronger self-awareness. She felt she could do as she pleased and didn't want anyone telling her what to do. This created friction between the two who already had a difficult, challenging relationship, and the socialite friends avoided each other for many months.

Coco felt powerful, maybe for the first time in her life, she felt that she had control over herself and everything else; and now, with her new hobby as a patron for many artists in Paris, she also had some level of control over some of the most important artists of the time. It is not difficult to understand what drew together Paris' most famous designer and the charismatic Russian composer; many believe that Stravinsky was going through a difficult, challenging phase at the time and that he welcomed Coco's interest as well as her help and support; he found in Coco a friend, a powerful friend and that friendship quickly turned into a love affair.

Stravinsky was born near St. Petersburg, Russia, in 1882. His whole family came from a strong musical background, both his parents were, in fact, very musical with his father being one of the leading Russian operatic basses of his day while his mother was a famous pianist. He started studying music at a very young age, and he specialised in piano and music theory. He also graduated with a law and philosophy degree from St. Petersburg University. Despite having studied music and coming from a family of musicians, he did not become fully aware of his talent until 1902 when he was taken as a private student by composer Nikolai Rimsky-Korsakov who not only became a tutor but also his spiritual guide. Nikolai was a Russian composer and teacher who had fame and success after producing some highly descriptive orchestrations. Korsakov was one of the few teachers to teach two different generations of talented Russian composers, including Stravinsky who was his student for many years. Korsakov was so highly sought after as a teacher that his music textbooks *His Practical Manual of Harmony* (published in 1884) and *Fundamentals of Orchestration* (published in 1913) are still used in Russia.

Under Korsakov's directions, Stravinsky did not attend the conservatory and never received an academic training; however, what he did get was tutoring in orchestration by Korsakov who also had him perform in his student weekly meetings. Korsakov strongly believed that Stravinsky had a unique talent which he thought could be damaged by a too rigorous education, and being conscious of how rare his talent was, decided to do anything in his power to protect that.

His lack of technical musical training probably had an impact on Coco, but what drew her to him in the first place, was that despite his years of practice, Stravinsky's talent could still have quite a rough side; Coco who had taught herself how to sew with creativity and how to go up and beyond, becoming a successful business woman must have felt a real connection with the Russian composer. And the bond between them was so powerful that it couldn't be contained, not even by the fact that Stravinsky's wife and children were living under the same roof.

In 1909 a pivotal meeting in the life of Stravinsky completely changed his creative career. He met theatre businessman Serge Diaghilev who had attended a concert in St. Petersburg featuring *Scherzo*, an early orchestral piece by Stravinsky. Diaghilev was so impressed with the Russian composer that he asked him to come and work for him; he had some orchestral arrangements that he needed for the summer season of the Ballet Russes in Paris; a ballet company that would in the future also see Coco Chanel's involvement as a costume designer. Stravinsky and Diaghilev established a long-lasting partnership which saw them work together several times. In 1910, they collaborated on the music of his *Firebird* which opened at the Paris Opera and turned Stravinsky into one of the most successful composers of his time. Stranvisky and Diaghilev also worked together the following year, in 1911, once again, for the Ballet Russes.

It was a strong, creative moment for Stravinsky, he was looking into himself more and, especially, looking for the right way to channel his creativity. After working with Diaghilev, he started to think about the possibility of crafting a more innovative production, something that would echo of paganism, and could potentially excite and confuse the audience at the same time. He created *The Rite of Spring*. The choreography, music and plot were all so suggestive and daring, shocking the audience and fuelling protests; this production made Stravinsky known as the composer behind the success and even the turmoil behind *The Rite of Spring*, something that made him take the distance from his motherland more and more and make Paris his new home.

After his success in Paris, he brought his wife Catherine and their children to France but with the outbreak of The First World War, he soon found himself with no job, with the Ballet Russes performances being halted, and with no country to go back to as following the Russian Revolution of 1917. His wife and cousin, Catherine Nossenko was a musician herself and she and Igor had known each other since childhood; they had got married in the village of Omelne in the mansion of Dmytro Nosenko after falling in love at first sight with Catherine inspiring several of Stravinsky's best works; there was never any doubt about Stravinsky loving his wife and considering her the true love of his life.

With not much left, he and his family had moved to Switzerland and stayed there until the end of the war. The Russian Revolution had an impact on many people; after the losses of The First World War and with the country being in poverty with food and first necessities becoming more and more scarce, Russia entered a crisis which culminated in the revolution and in the assassination of the tsar and his family.

Stravinsky and his family left Switzerland in 1920 and lived in France with Coco for a few months, starting a mysterious affair which scandalised public opinion. After attending the premiere of *The Rite of Spring*, Coco found herself mesmerised with the Russian composer, she was captivated and interested in meeting the man who was behind such an innovative, artistic production. After all, Coco was a pioneer even in her way of thinking, she saw talent and genius where other people saw confusion and disruption. They didn't meet straightaway, Coco tried but Stravinsky was in no mood to meet new people or chat to anyone; they would not meet for seven years after that, Stravinsky needed time to recover himself after what the production had done to his reputation.

By then, Stravinsky and his family were living in poverty at the time, and Coco, who had been taken with the composer for many years, decided to invite him and his family to come and stay in her villa not far from Paris, in Garches. They moved to the villa straightaway and Stravinsky reluctantly accepted Coco's help; moving there with his four children.

At Coco's, Stravinsky had at his disposal a separate room with a very expensive piano where he could finally focus on his music; they became lovers quite easily and effortlessly, it did not matter that Stravinsky's wife was staying in the same house, it did not represent an issue at all. Coco wanted the musician and Stravinsky could not refuse her; they were a couple of artists who loved spending time together. His wife accepted the new situation and decided to keep the affair a secret, she was grateful to Coco for taking care of her family and decided to play along, as painful as it was.

Once in Paris, Stravinsky and his family had led a life very different to the one they had been used to. They had lost all their properties in Russia during the revolution and they were barely surviving; Catherine was grateful to Coco and her help despite everything else.

Talking later about Coco, Stravinsky would say that she was a woman of many talents: beautiful, feminine and, absolutely perfect but he equally made sure to admit that he had never felt enough for her. Even after leaving Coco's villa, the composer kept accepting financial help from Coco who would send money to support his work and his family; they stayed friends but their passion was gone and despite having spent several months together, Coco never inspired any of the Russian composer's work.

It is a mystery to understand if they met again after those months of passion; many say that Coco and Stravinsky met years later to share memories of those beautiful times spent together while others believe that they never met again.

When talking to Morand about Stravinsky, Coco said that he had pursued her, claiming that she had tried to stop the affair from the very beginning, but that Stravinsky could not be dissuaded. She never mentioned or used the word love, but she talked about a mutual attraction and most importantly, she also mentioned Misia and her husband Jojo's interference in the affair. To Morand, Coco admitted that she had been supporting the musician financially, even paying for Stravinsky to perform at the Salle Gaveau and, with pride, she took credit for the positive impact she had had on the composer's music and productions; she really believed that she had given him the right inspiration and motivation to accomplish things he would not have been capable to achieve without her. As for Misia and Jojo Sert's mingling in her affair, she said the couple was always interfering in peoples' lives and their supposed concern was simply a way of controlling Coco.

Coco and Grand Duke Dmitri Pavlovich

Coco told Morand that while she had been entangled in the affair with the Russian composer, she had also decided to meet her longtime friend Grand Duke Dmitri Pavlovich of Russia with whom she decided to go to Monte Carlo with; even then, she kept saying to Morand that everything was very friendly and that there was no malice in her attitude; despite many researchers saying quite the opposite and accusing Coco of having a second relationship on the side with the Grand Duke himself.

Grand Duke Dmitri was another fascinating character in Coco's universe, he was one of the few Romanovs to escape the revolution with his successors being able to see the restoration of the Alexander Palace; he is rumoured to have escaped the revolution because he had been one of the men behind the plot to murder Rasputin, and that is exactly why he had been sent by his uncle Nicholas to join an army unit in Persia. From there, he ran away to England and the United States. He was often described as being a carefree, young man and that is what might have attracted Coco in the first place.

Dmitri was born in 1891 and he was the only son of Princess Alexandra of Greece and Grand Duke Paul Alexandrovich. His mother died in childbirth and Dmitri and his older sister Marie Pavlovna went to live with their uncle and auntie, Grand Duke Sergei and Grand Duchess Elizabeth, the couple was not parent material and it was rumoured that they had no children of their own because of Sergei's homosexuality. Dmitri grew up attached to the Grand Duchess who was the closest thing he had to a mother. He did not have much of a relationship with his father and after he remarried a divorcee called Olga Karnovich, he had three other children, and he and Dmitri became more distant. Later in her life, his beloved aunt Elizabeth would become a nun, something which probably had an effect on Dmitri and something too that may have resonated with Coco who had been raised by nuns herself at Aubazine. Many researchers, including Lisa Davidson, speculated that Dmitri was raised by his cousin Nicholas, the tsar, and that he spent most of his time living at the Alexander Palace with the rest of the Romanov family; after all, Alexander was about 20 years older than him and could have been the closest thing Dmitri had to a father figure.

Both Dmitri and Coco had been abandoned by those they loved the most and most importantly by those who were supposed to take care of them. Dmitri lost his whole family during the Russian Revolution as well as his aunt, Elizabeth who was murdered only a few days after entering the convent where she had chosen to spend the rest of her days as a nun. Death was a recurring theme in Dmitri's life as much as in Coco's, they experienced the deaths of those they loved so suddenly and abruptly, and they decided to stop suffering because of that; becoming almost accustomed to the idea of death, and almost, completely indifferent to it all. Nicholas had grown fond of Dmitri and he had wanted him to marry his eldest daughter, Olga; however, Olga did not want an arranged marriage as she wanted to fall in love, much like her parents had done, and she not only refused Dmitri but also other cousins including Boris Vladimirovich and Prince Carol of Romania.

Dmitri's involvement in Rasputin's death has been marked by mysterious and blurry details; later, he would swear that he had nothing to do with the affair. Yet Rasputin was not a loved and respected figure in Russia, and he was rumoured to have supernatural powers; his influence on both Nicholas and Alexandra had made them lose their authority and credibility not only in the eyes of the Russian people but also with their own family. After the Russian Revolution took away his family, Dmitri married an American woman, heiress Audrey Emery, in Biarritz, a place he would often even visit with Coco as well.

When talking to Morand later in her life, Coco swore that the idea of going to Monte Carlo had been sudden and natural; Dmitri and Coco were just friends and not lovers. That night, having a very spontaneous moment, Coco decided to go to Monte Carlo with him, straight after dinner, without thinking twice about Stravinsky or what anyone else would think. Rumour has it that Misia sent a telegram to Stravinsky telling him that Coco and Dmitri were off to Monte Carlo as a couple, something which she always fervently denied. According to Coco, it was Misia who begged her to come back to Paris as Stravinsky had, apparently, gone mad with jealousy. The truth was that after this episode, Coco and Stravinsky broke up, and the Russian musician then went through a deep religious conversion, creating many compositions in Latin, and working with Diaghilev again on some of his most famous productions including the *Pulcinella*.

Many people claimed that Coco had exaggerated her love with Stravinsky in her conversations with Morand, and that there was no relationship to begin with, but just a little affair she had blown up out of proportions for extra publicity.

Stravinsky's second wife Vera De Bosset would just say that Chanel had just used her husband's name to brag about her love life; after the musician's death. De Bosset had grown extremely protective of Stravinsky's legacy with many details emerging after her own death, as reported in an obituary by the *New York Times*.

De Bosset died in her Fifth Avenue apartment in New Year at 93 years old; despite having lost her husband when she was already in her 80s, she had become extremely well-known to the public after Stravinsky's death; mainly because of rumours surrounding Stravinsky's will and whether the document had been marked as authentic or not. De Bosset had also been the object of controversies with regards to the authenticity of some of the new music published after her husband's death and the disposition of his estate.

The will itself had been signed a year and four months before Stravinsky's death and it specifically stated that the Russian musician had left everything he owned to Vera and that only after Vera's death, would everything eventually go to his children or any other heirs. A part of his fortune was also going to Robert Craft who had been Stravinsky's left hand for over twenty years and was also a writer and conductor. Many rumoured that Stravinsky's works published after his death were in fact Craft's works but just published under Stravinsky's name so that they could live off the Russian musician's fame. These claims were also published in a book written by Lillian Libman, Stravinsky's representative during the last decade of his life.

Vera also got herself into a dispute with Stravinsky's three surviving children and a granddaughter; their claims were that Vera had not only misappropriated Stravinsky's assets but was also now using his name and publicity to make more money with the books. The dispute ended with Stravinsky's children winning and being involved in the administration of the estate and other concessions. Vera married Stravinsky in Bedford where he was lecturing at Harvard University and in a later interview, she admitted that they had had a long affair for twenty years before marrying after being first introduced by Diaghilev in a restaurant in Montmartre. Stravinsky decided to start an affair with Vera and insisted on his wife meeting her; Catherine had tuberculosis but did not die until 1939; many researchers found that the two women became friends and thought highly of each other. Before marrying Stravinsky, Vera worked in an atelier designing and making costumes; and, she was, also, a supervisor for a fashion accessories shop called the Tula-Vera; which sold artificial flowers. Many believe that Vera was very jealous of Coco; she had similar interests and skills to Coco, but she never found the same approval or success; she worked on costumes for Diaghilev, was a socialite and lived off her own work but she never reached Coco's level. She became Stravinsky's lover, benefitted from Catherine's approval, yet she never became, much to her chagrin, a new Coco Chanel.

Chanel and Westminster

Coco's affair with Dmitri lasted three years and many people including the painter Marie Laurencin believed that Coco had married him in secret. However, they weren't actually destined to stay together. Coco was by then a true icon in the fashion world, her designs were on the cover of important fashion magazines like *Vogue* and *Harper's Bazaar,* and she had finally turned into the romantic heroine she had always wanted to be; loved, envied and admired by everyone but most importantly, she had succeeded in becoming financially independent from any man, something that allowed her to end relationships and affairs when she pleased.

She was entering into a new phase in her life: she was finally a highly sought member of Parisian society, a patron, someone who could both inspire and help artists; and soon, more and more influential people started to realise that. The Duke of Westminster had recently separated from his first wife, Constance, and was having dinner in Paris at the Ritz Hotel with a small circle of friends including Vera Bates, a very good friend of Coco, when he met the up and coming designer for the first time.

Coco was still in a relationship with Dmitri and was not looking for love, she knew how frail men's egos were and could not be bothered with another man in her life. She was a little cautious as well, as she was used to artists and people from a more high-class circle, but she had never been in a relationship with royalty before (Westminster was a cousin of George V). In 1924, Coco decided to take a break from Paris and invited Vera to spend the Christmas holiday with her in Monte Carlo, she was feeling strangely lonely, despite having everything she needed: money, fame, power, someone who loved her. It was this sense that something was missing that opened the door to Westminster.

In Monte Carlo, Westminster invited Vera, Coco and later Dmitri to have dinner with him on his yacht, *The Flying Cloud*, afterwards they went to the casino, playing all night. Following that very first meeting, Westminster was so taken by Coco that he started a persistent courtship;

he would do anything to grab her attention, sending flowers, fresh salmon he had fished himself, letters, and beautiful baskets of fruits – anything to conquer the heart of the French Mademoiselle.

Eventually, Coco, a romantic at heart, caved in and started a romantic affair with Westminster; after all, she was very mystical and believed in destiny; and she had known for quite some time that another man would have come into her life and make her happy again; and this man turned out to be the Duke of Westminster or as his close friends loved to call him, Bend'Or, after his grandfather's stallion, winner of the 1880 Derby. Once an adult, many friends, including Winston Churchill, would just call him 'Bendor' or 'Benny'.

At the time, Westminster was separated from his second wife, Violet Mary Nelson; although, many people believe that the two were still very much together when his affair with Coco started; it was not the first time Westminster had been unfaithful to his wife but that was one of the reasons she had filed for divorce after only five years of marriage. A tall man, with blue eyes and a restless attitude to life, Westminster was someone who was used to having everything he wanted and would not take no for an answer, not even from a worldwide loved and respected fashion icon. Their affair lasted ten years and was everything Coco had read about in her books, and in her novels as a teenager; the couple would spend time at Westminster's different properties including his Sutherland estate at Stack Lodge and other properties at Lochmore in Scotland, or on his yacht.

While staying in Lochmore, Coco became an expert fisherwoman which found even the appreciation of Winston Churchill himself; in his letters to his wife, Churchill praised Coco and her endless talents several times. This was not surprising of course. Coco had a talent for any sport she tried; years before she had taught herself how to ride while staying at Balsan's, she had decided that she was never going to be any less than her lovers or her friends, and if there was something she didn't know how to do, she would just learn. Lochmore was a beautiful Victorian building which Coco loved, it was the perfect location for her romantic narrative, and she must have thought, the perfect ending to all her love and life tribulations.

Westminster was so in love with this particular part of Scotland that he also bought Rosehall, another estate in Sutherland, which had previously been owned by William Ewing Gilmour, a businessman. The couple spent several months together in Rosehall where Coco became exceptional at fishing; the property is, to this very day, the only house in Britain to be styled and decorated by Coco. Coco was incredibly inspired by Scotland and so were her collections; particularly her tweed designs were believed to have been influenced by the duke's fishing and hunting gear.

Westminster was often described as being childish and temperamental. He did not tolerate adultery, but both his marriages had ended because of him being unfaithful to his wives. Coco saw her relationship with Westminster as a nice change, especially after having relationships with men who needed her help, both financially and emotionally; and she found in Westminster someone who could finally give her the life she deserved. Westminster did not need any financial help, he had been in the world long enough to have reached some sort of emotional balance and he could take care of her like no one, probably not even Capel, had ever done before. If with Capel, she had had to fight her way through by imposing her presence during social events, knowing for a fact that he was not thrilled with her presence in his social circle, with Westminster, she was exactly where she had to be, maybe for the first time in her life; she had become a fashion icon, everyone was wearing Chanel and she was perfectly suited and positively embraced by all his friends, including Churchill who was absolutely taken by the French Mademoiselle. Churchill admired Coco so much that he described her in one of his letters to his wife as being one of the strongest personalities he had ever seen with Westminster; he was particularly fond of Coco's hunting skills as well as her booming fashion business and how she so capably managed to take care of everything.

Westminster was so in love with Coco that he asked her several times to marry him, but that she refused him every time, the same way she had refused Capel and Balsan. Rumour has it that the duke was so infatuated that he had every single lamppost in Westminster engraved with the Chanel symbol so that when she was far, back to Paris, to take care of her business, he would still have a little Chanel in London.

The only thing Westminster did not like about Coco was the fact that she would not leave her business behind and move to London with him; so in 1927, they reached a compromise and Coco opened a boutique on Davies Street in London's Mayfair; the boutique was lent to her by Westminster. Soon, she began mixing with the British circle, dressing some of the most important women of the time including Bada d'Erlanger, the Marquise de Cast Maury, Lady Mary Davies, Lady Northcliffe and many more. Many people wondered why Westminster liked Coco so much and the truth was that she did not need him, she was not trying to marry him, and she did not need his money or power; she had both. They were two people, two adults, who would spend many years together, attracting the interest of both the French and British society of the time, but who didn't need each other. From his side, Westminster was looking for a wife and a new heir, he had two daughters and no son and was still mourning the death of his little boy Edward who had died of appendicitis at the age of four. He was an independent man and he was not ready to compromise who he was; whoever he married next needed to be an open-minded, modern, independent woman who, in a nutshell, would have let him be unfaithful to her on a regular basis.

Coco was a modern woman and could have fit the bill; she could have been the perfect wife but she might have had some difficulties in giving him an heir as she was now in her forties; many believe that she tried everything in her power to give Westminster a son but she could not get pregnant. Many biographers and researchers believe that a previous abortion after an unwanted pregnancy with Balsan or Capel had made it impossible for her to have a child. This put a strain on her relationship with Westminster, she had chosen to believe in their romantic love story, but she could not give him a child and despite trying, she could not love him the way she had loved Capel.

Despite their differences and their growing issues regarding Coco not being able to get pregnant, Coco and Westminster had the most extravagant yet fulfilling life together. Not long after the start of their romance, Westminster gave Coco an amazing apartment in Mayfair and bought her the most beautiful jewels as well as expensive gifts and paintings. In 1927, he decided to give her the deed to a land he had acquired on the French Riviera; it was a one of a kind, French villa she named La Pausa which means 'pause' in Italian. La Pausa shared some interior features with Aubazine something which had inspired Coco for her entire life.

Eventually, Westminster married someone else, someone who understandably was not a Chanel fan. Her name was Loelia Ponsonby, and she was born in 1902 and was the only daughter of the courtier Sir Frederick Ponsonby; after a childhood spent at St James's Palace, Park House at Sandringham and Birkhall, Loelia joined the Bright Young People, a group of young people who would pull pranks impersonating reporters and securing interviews from famous people. She was a socialite and apparently the inventor of the bottle party, where guests would bring their own drink to the party. She and Westminster married in 1930 with Churchill as a best man; the marriage was not a successful one as Loelia couldn't cope with Westminster's mood swings which went from generous, showering his new wife with jewels and affection to fits of cruelty, they divorced shortly afterwards. Westminster and Coco remained friends for the rest of their lives, with Coco admitting that she had loved him or at least thought she had loved him.

Coco and Iribe

Coco had several affairs throughout her life, she loved artists and would often surround herself with them, finding inspiration in their artistry, wit and genius. She was muse and inspired several artists, including Picasso, who later became one of her closest friends.

There is a famous picture of a very chic Coco Chanel with her unmissable hat posing with a group of friends; the friends are most certainly posing, Coco is smiling, and she is looking at Paul Iribe, mesmerised with infatuation, the smile only a muse would give to his favourite artist.

Born in 1883 in Angoulême, France, Iribe was a newspaper typographer and illustrator for different French publications including *Le Temps*, and he was also one of the creative minds who created the satirical journal, *Le Témoin*. His extraordinary work grabbed the attention of fashion designer Paul Poiret who insisted on having Iribe to work on illustrations to accompany his first dress collection; later, Iribe also published a limited edition of 250 copies of collections of fashion illustrations under the name *Les robes de Paul Poiret,* it was a success, Iribe's collection grabbed the attention of the public and the media alike for its bright colours and the use of Japanese prints. The collection also perfectly embodied all the changes the fashion world was going through, especially, with a more fitted silhouette becoming the new trend. Coco and Iribe had many things in common, including a love for the arts and for fashion, something that formed the basis of their relationship.

Iribe also worked as a decorator, cartoonist and art director. His career as an illustrator had started when he was only 17 and he freelanced for different papers including *L'Assiette au Beurre Rire*, and *Sourire*. Iribe was deeply influenced by the art deco movement, something which he tried to bring to his illustrations for the fashion world. In 1919, he moved to New York where he gained further acknowledgement from a more innovative, modern audience which was fascinated by his take on art deco with the result of his work being published in the American edition of *Vogue*.

He opened two stores, one in New York and one in Paris. Iribe also worked with the fashion designer Jeanne Parquin, much to Coco's annoyance, creating for her a similar collection of illustrations. Iribe moved back to Paris in 1933 and was awarded La Légion d'honneur, he began to work on different projects which included books, furniture design, jewellery and fashion. He met Coco through mutual friends and the two started a romantic affair, she became his muse and he started to draw more and more women who looked like her for *Le Témoin*. The couple also partnered together for the creation of a jewellery collection sponsored by the house of Chanel. Their romance didn't last long and Iribe died of a heart attack while he was staying at one of Coco's villas.

Coco and Reverdy

Coco met Pierre Reverdy through one of her famous friends and rumoured lovers, Pablo Picasso. It looks like Misia had managed to protect her, or so she thought, from Picasso, but she could do nothing to protect her from Reverdy, and she really should have.

After moving to Paris at the beginning of 1900, Reverdy decided to become a poet following the death of his father, who had always been a positive, supportive figure in his life. During that time, Reverdy was forced to try and live off his writing. His first collection of poems was published in 1915 marking the beginning of a prolific and rewarding poetry career, and not surprisingly, he became one of the many personalities to gravitate around Coco while also being friends with some of the most influential people in French society including Guillaume Apollinaire, Max Jacob, Pablo Picasso, Juan Gris and Georges Braque. By associating himself with these artists, Reverdy became one of the most inspiring members and exponents of cubism and surrealism; inspired by these movements, he created and founded a monthly review called *Nord-Sud* in 1917 which brought together both artistic approaches for the first time.

The review succeeded in featuring many highly regarded authors of the time including Apollinaire, Jacob, Louis Aragon, André Breton and Philippe Soupault. His maximum recognition as a poet arrived later in 1924 when Reverdy published *Les Epaves Du Ciel*; this showed his influence on cubism and surrealism. Surrealist people started to sing his praises for the lonely, slightly anxious tone of his work while cubist artists particularly loved his short yet fragmented poems. Despite being highly influenced by both movements, Reverdy managed to remain independent and declared his total absence of preference. He tried to focus on what he called being the true reality with his writing assuming mystical tones, something which Coco must have been pretty drawn to. According to several researchers, his work tried to move past reality and its superficiality and go deeper beyond its meaning. He believed that the reality and its truth were being concealed and that poetry was the only way to unveil that; by getting himself involved in this mystical and spiritual journey, he decided to embrace Catholicism and in 1926, he retired to an ascetic life close to the Benedictine monastery at Solesmes. He spent the rest of his life there devoting himself to his poetry and religion.

In her book, Lisa Chaney suggested that Coco and Reverdy fell in love because they felt a little disengaged from the world. Coco never felt like she fully belonged; she had friends, she was a patron for many artists, she was always involved in their lives, always at their sides when they needed but most of them, but she never felt truly part of society. Reverdy was famous for his erratic behaviour, which often went from him adoring Coco to being repulsed by her, due to his guilt about his wife. She did what she did best, she helped him financially, bought his manuscripts, encouraged him and pushed him to do better but his asceticism had already started to expand and take control of his life, something she could do almost nothing about. He had a wife and felt guilty about cheating on her but that did not stop him from having several affairs.

Reverdy was also famous for his fits of rage, and he lost many of his friends who could not understand his sudden mood swings. Soon enough, his visits to Coco's house became less and less frequent and he decided to embrace a simpler life, going to live in a tiny house not far from the Benedictine Abbey of Solesmes.

Coco and Reverdy stayed friends their entire life, it was not in Coco's style to forget about her lovers once they stopped being that. They had found common ground in their simple origins, in their bucolic past. Neither felt completely accepted by their eclectic circle of artists and highly sought personalities of the time; they felt estranged from them despite attending their parties, functions and generally being a part of their glamorous world. It was this sense of alienation that drew them together. Reverdy chose a more solitary, ascetic life to the one offered in Paris, and Coco, alone again, decided to focus on her business and became what everyone knew and loved – an icon and possibly a spy.

Chapter 7

Coco, the Spy

In our collective imaginary, a spy, any spy, is always beautiful, smart and incredibly well-connected. She often speaks several languages and can be quite ruthless if anything stands in her way. Beautiful, focused and well-connected – no wonder so many people thought Coco could perfectly fit the bill of the perfect spy. To this day, there is still a mystery surrounding her involvement with the Nazis.

Hal Vaughan, in his book, *Sleeping with the Enemy*, made several claims about Coco being a spy and working for the Nazis during the Second World War. These claims were quickly dismissed by the house of Chanel; referring to such powerful allegations, a spokesperson stressed how Coco befriended many Jewish people during her life including the Rothschild family, the photographer Irving Penn and Joseph Kessel, a French writer.

Despite such a bold statement from the house of Chanel itself, the rumours and allegations have never really stopped, and many believe that during the Second World War, Coco was an intermediary between the Allies and the Germans working on establishing a settlement between the nations, known as *Operation Modelhut*. Becoming a Nazi spy was not something that just occurred by chance and according to many, was ignited by Coco's deep anti-Semitism. In his book, Vaughan stressed how Coco felt she had been robbed of her profits during her 20-year legal action against the Wertheimer brothers for Chanel N°5; Vaughan pointed out that far from being pushed from her economic interests and far from being robbed in the first place, Coco was mainly driven by her anti-Semitic ideals. The problem was not how much she was making from Chanel N°5, the issue was not, as she had expressed, the ingredients being of scarce quality and Coco being worried about her customers; the main issue here was that the brothers were Jewish and Coco, much like some of her most famous beloved friends, including Paul Morand, was an anti-Semite.

But what had exactly happened with the Wertheimer brothers?

In 1922, before the start of the Second World War, Coco had met Pierre Wertheimer, director of the Bourjois perfume and cosmetics company. Wertheimer was no stranger to the cosmetics business, as his father Ernest had previously invested in Bourjois. Wertheimer and Coco had several things in common including a passion for horse riding which had led The Wertheimers to get involved in the racing business more and more seriously. It was, after all, one day at the races that Wertheimer met Mademoiselle Chanel, with their acquaintance quickly becoming a partnership. They were both interested in making the most of the trend of the time which saw designers, fashion designers and accessory designers expanding into the cosmetics business and launching their own perfumes. Coco knew that her fragrance, the Chanel fragrance, had to be just perfect, from the ingredients to the packaging and marketing strategy to represent her and what the Chanel house stood for. The perfume became a success, a trend, an icon, women who wore Chanel were rebels and knew who they were. Chanel was on everyone's lips, her name echoed of anything that was new, revolutionary and womanly; she had become an icon.

Pierre and Coco were introduced by Théophile Bader, a businessman who was also the co-founder of the Galeries Lafayette. Bader was the connection between Wertheimer and Chanel, he was interested in selling Chanel at his store and would have done anything in his power to do so.

At the time, Chanel N°5 was still produced in small quantities and in Ernest Beau's labs; it was good, but it wasn't enough for Coco and Bader. They wanted to start producing the fragrance on a larger scale and in order to do so, they needed a partner, an influential, trustworthy one. A deal was quickly negotiated between the three, with N°5 being made in Wertheimer's Bourjois factory; Wertheimer quickly became the main partner earning seventy per cent of the profits; Bader earned twenty per cent as a middle man, while Coco, despite having been the one to have the idea, received only ten per cent of any profit made. Coco was not happy about the situation, she felt it was not right as she had been the one to come up with the idea and the product in the first place; she also felt that the ingredients used at the Bourjois factory were not of the best quality and that would eventually devalue her product which had taken years to come together; many chose to believe that any problem with the Wertheimer was of a different nature; the family was Jewish and Coco was accused of being an anti-Semite.

With the start of the lawsuit and the beginning of the Second World War, the partnership became inevitably compromised; Madsen in his biography said that Wertheimer had lawyers just to deal with Chanel and her lawsuit. When Paris was occupied by the Nazis, the Wertheimer brothers fled to New York not before going to Grasse to get the Chanel N°5 formula so that they could reproduce the fragrance once safe in America. The lawsuit survived the Second World War, and dragged on for years, with Coco even threatening a new production of a different version, her own version of Chanel N°5, something which she never did. Eventually, they settled and in spite of everything, the lawsuit, the war, the anti-Semite accusation, whatever had happened, they got back to being friends and business partners again.

Trouble came in the shape of a man during the Paris occupation of the Second World War. Coco was rumoured to have started a relationship with Baron Hans Gunther von Dincklage who apparently worked very closely with Nazi propaganda minister Joseph Goebbels, the right-hand man to Hitler. The timing of her relationship with Dincklage was not as convenient as it looked and many believe that the pair had started their romantic affair way before the war and stayed together even after that; however, according to biographer Hal Vaughan, during the war, Coco did not only become a Nazi spy but also ended up playing a far more important role in the war itself.

When it came to Dincklage, Coco would say that the pair had known each other way before the war and then for over twenty years. According to Coco's biographer, Hal Vaughan, Dincklage was an Abwehr (German military intelligence) agent who was working under Hitler and had received the order to work directly for Berlin. Coco, who had been forced to close some of her business because of both the war and the Great Depression, had become involved with Dincklage maybe, at first, to maintain some sort of authority, even during the war; in a way, to still be Coco Chanel, when most people had been denied the right to be themselves.It is interesting to notice that Coco was not the kind of person who would lose or like to lose to anyone, let alone the Germans, so she managed to keep some dignity during such a difficult time.

To maintain some level of power or authority, Coco, allegedly, found herself involved in a relationship with someone who would be of help to her during such unpredictable times; someone who could be, once again, a good connection. Thanks to her relationship with Dincklage, she managed to keep some level of independence during what was starting to look like a different world to the one she had been used to. She was granted special permission to stay in her apartment at the Ritz in Paris which also served as German military headquarters during the German occupation of Paris.

Coco fell in love with Dincklage at the age of 57, he would be the last of her love affairs or the last of her known love affairs. He was the most controversial of all her lovers yet he was the perfect romantic hero; a strong man who could be of help to her during the war, she also relished not having to support her partner financially or having to embrace his artistry; that must have felt like a nice change for someone who had been a patron and lover to many creative minds of the time.

She fell in love with Dincklage at a time where she was losing a little of herself, the Chanel in her; her boutiques had been shut down by the Great Depression, and her perfume, the one she had invented, the one only she with her particular talent and sensitivity could have ever conceived, was not completely her own. She was also not young anymore and for someone who had lived the perfect life of the romantic heroine, getting old must have been the worst punishment ever. Most importantly, André Palasse, her nephew, Julia's son, had been captured by the Germans and was now in a labour camp. André was the only family she had left or the only family she cared about; she could not bear the thought of losing him and she would do anything in her power to get him back safely home. She had known from her German sources that André was not doing well and that he was sick, and maybe had tuberculous; she knew she had to get him out of there, and that there was no time to waste. For someone who had always been told that she lacked maternal instincts and was accused of being cold, she certainly showed the determination of a mother when it came to getting André back.

Many believe that she was only partly motivated by love, the love for her nephew, and for Gabrielle, her great-niece, André's daughter; many believed that she was also motivated by power; she had lost so much already, everything she had worked for, her entire life, she was not someone who liked to lose, and, definitely, not someone who was used to not getting her way. She was granted access to a Ritz suite and her relationship with Dincklage allowed her into some of the forbidden areas in Paris. She could also travel while so many could not.

Yet, she was desperate to get André back, and she decided to use her influence with Dincklage and with German double agent Baron Louis de Vaufreland; the Baron's boss had agreed to meet Coco and assured her that he would not only get André Palasse out of the concentration camp he had been imprisoned in but would also help her with her legal action for Chanel N°5. However, she had to do something in return. In order to receive Nazi support, she was allegedly asked to show her support to the German regime, by using her fame, reputation and connections to help their cause; that is how she, allegedly, agreed to make a trip with Vaufreland to Madrid to try and help the Germans to secure political information. According to several records found by Vaughn, Coco made that trip to Madrid twice. The first time she went under the false pretence of opening a Spanish boutique in Madrid; here she accompanied Vaufreland, and according to several records, the assignment was an ongoing German military intelligence mission to recruit men and women and convince them to become spies to serve the Nazi regime. The Abwehr made sure to enrol Coco with a number, her name was 'Westminster' as a reference to Bendor, her former lover.

Was this a clear way to prove her loyalty to the Nazis so that she could get André back home before it was too late? Or had she really turned her back on the French people and fully embraced the Nazi regime and cause?

During the occupation, Coco had maintained a good relationship with German soldiers and had been the one to ensure André Palasse's return home. She had a German lover, she had more access than she had ever had before, and, clearly, at least on the surface, she was not hating the Nazi occupation.

How she felt about anti-Semitism remains a mystery. Was she really that intolerant towards Jewish people? Was she that indifferent to Jewish children being deported as it was later reported?

After the liberation of Paris in August 1944, a weight had been lifted from the French people's shoulders; their city had been freed and the Germans were gone; four years of continuous humiliation and literally being told what to do and where to go in their own country had finally come to an end, they were finally free. They could have been happy, enjoying the liberation and celebrating a half-victory; instead the French pride kicked in and they decided to start what would then be called an epuration phase; this phase aimed to get rid of all those French who had not fought for France and had instead chosen to collaborate with the Germans; women who had become lovers of French soldiers and anyone who had collaborated with the regime. People were dragged off the street, murdered, and often raped; it was not a pleasant show, and it was a brutal way, to start afresh. Many had suffered under the German rules and several wanted to remove the cancer some French people had brought to their very own cities, betraying their own.

Coco Chanel was no different. She knew the French pride; she had invented the French pride and she knew they would come for her as well.

Coco was brought in for questioning but released only a few hours later thanks to the intervention of her friend, Winston Churchill. She left for Switzerland and Dincklage followed later. Coco was now 61.

Unlike Coco, not many people suspected of treason were spared and the new government established by Charles De Gaulle sentenced to death any traitor found guilty; Vichy chief Philippe Pétain and his prime minister, Pierre Laval, were the first to be tried with Laval being sentenced and shot. During this phase of purge, over 160,000 cases were tried in court and over 7,000 people were sentenced to death; but only 1,500 were actually executed with most sentences being spent in prison. Two years after the liberation of Paris, Coco was brought before French authorities once again; it was 1946 and Judge Roger Serre demanded a full analysis of her activities during the time of the war. Her cooperation with the Germans and her relationship with Baron Louis de Vaufreland were scrutinised. Vaufreland was also brought in for interrogation and it was him who told the authorities about Coco's involvement, about their travel to Madrid; how it had been an espionage mission. Vaufreland told Serre that Coco had become a Nazi spy and had joined him as a cover for his intelligence work. During her interrogations, Coco called Vaufreland's ideas absolutely delusional and not based on facts. She was just a businesswoman who looked like the perfect spy because of her connections and extensive travel for work.

The evidence against Coco was inconclusive, and she was released. Later, according to Vaughn, Serre found out that Coco had undertaken a second mission to Madrid for SS General Walter Schellenberg, Himmler's chief of SS intelligence; he also learnt that Dincklage himself had been a German military intelligence officer: Abwehr agent F-8680.

Despite rumours about Coco being a spy and several biographies and articles published around that theme, she was never charged, and after being interrogated, she was fully discharged of any accusation of having worked as a Nazi collaborator. Her name had been cleared but her reputation remained tainted, and it had become apparent that she was not welcome in Paris anymore. She had become a traitor, that is why she exiled herself to Switzerland and lived in her country house in Roquebrune for a while, taking some time to recharge and think about her next move.

Chapter 8

Coco, the Friend

There is always a party going on, not necessarily involving alcohol, but there is always a party, a group of several people gathering together and celebrating something, a new collaboration, a birthday, life.

She usually stands in the middle or at the side as if she is looking at the scene from a distance, she joins in, but she never really does for real. In all the photographs, I have seen and researched of Coco Chanel, it is more than likely to find her in the company of her friends, some of them were not at all that close to her of course, yet she would find herself experiencing those years with some of the most interesting personalities of the time, feeding off each other's talent and ambition, entangling herself in acquaintances which turned into friendships and often romances. It would be impossible to tell Coco's story by only looking at her and not spending some time examining those who inspired her whole life.

One thing is for sure, Coco valued friendship. It was a different time of course, a time where you would spend hours at someone's place, arriving unannounced, losing yourself in intimate, often, whispered conversations; it was a time for artists who clearly did not have a nine to five work schedule and could spend endless hours discussing ideas, shows, new trends and politics often until dawn.

That was how you made friends at the time, something which became incredibly important to Coco, an orphan who had little or almost no family. With her name associated with several, incredibly well-known personalities of the time, it would be hard to imagine a world where she could have become Coco Chanel without her circle; her intimate yet fairly big circle of connections, acquaintances and yes, friends who were both adoring of her and intimidated by her mere presence.

In an interview several years ago, psychoanalyst Claude Delay, who is an author of a biography about Mademoiselle Chanel, often referred to Coco as her friend, her dear friend; Delay spent several years with Coco with Mademoiselle telling her all about her childhood as well as her life.

Morand, who also wrote about Coco, turning their conversations into a biography, was also known as one of Mademoiselle's closest friends.

But it was no easy task to become close to Coco. She was a shy creature, someone who used to hide during her fashion shows, who did not like to talk to journalists and who was rumoured to be prone to fits of anger.

It was no easy task to be liked by *la Mademoiselle* either. She was incredibly sensitive and intuitively knew whether someone was worthy of her trust and loyalty. Apparently, she was no stranger to jealousy, if she was close to someone, she would turn almost into a teenager and would not want to share that person with anyone else. She would become possessive and one might wonder how she survived Capel's numerous affairs or Balsan's. She was defensive and had a way of scrutinising people deeply before deciding whether she was interested in making their acquaintance or not.

Despite this, Coco was also remembered by her many friends as a kind creature; when she was your friend, her generosity would be uncontainable, she would shower the people she loved with affection and emotional and financial support, opening the door to almost endless possibilities.

She knew what it was like to come from nothing and she saw in many of her friends, her own challenges; the challenges of having grown up as an orphan, who did not come from a wealthy family and could not boast or, let alone, take advantage of any inherited fortune to fund her business; that is exactly why, in almost total absence of a supportive family, friends, connections and even lovers, became her everything and her inspiration behind her very own success. She had no powerful connections yet after leaving Aubazine, she managed to not only establish relationships and friendships with some of the most important people of the time, both French and worldwide but she also built a fashion empire, a brand and an icon from scratch. If it is true that it was a different time, a time perhaps where having the right connection was still a valuable currency, it is also true that Coco had inherited the charm from the best salesman she had ever known – her dad. From Samur to Aubazine, Paris and then later, the United States, many people came in contact with la Mademoiselle and some of them, succeeded in having a strong impact on Coco and her world in different yet interesting ways; much like the books she read, she was deeply touched by some of the best personalities of the time who would delicately gravitate around her and her subtle genius, a little like a hint of Chanel N°5. Some of her friends, if not all of them, were famous in their own right and went on to populate Coco's exclusive circle, their names ineluctably attached to hers.

Coco and Misia

One of these personalities, the source of both inspiration and continuous challenge, was Misia Sert.

Coco and Misia managed to establish a love-hate relationship which lasted their entire lives. Coco was not a big fan of women, something which changed later in her life when she strangely reconsidered the value of female friendship and would almost surrender herself with women, both models and friends, fuelling rumours of having become a lesbian. When she met Misia for the first time, shortly after Boy Capel's death, she was still not a big fan of women and preferred the company of men with whom she found she had more things in common. Despite this, Coco and Misia started an unlikely friendship which lasted for a lifetime with Misia playing an important role in Coco's life.

Misia remained Coco's only female friend for many years and despite the two of them losing touch after the Second World War, they kept gravitating around each other. As Morand writes in his book, Misia and Coco became friends just after Capel's tragic and sudden death, an episode which shook Coco to the core and threw her into a deep depression. By the time Coco and Misia met, Coco was not back to her usual self and was still knee-deep in her mourning phase. As Coco herself would explain to Morand later during their conversations, Misia was an eccentric character, a bold personality, who had been for many years the only female patron in her circle supporting artists and even modelling for them. She was also, according to Coco's memories, not as transparent as she claimed to be, and would often be attracted to other people, during their most difficult times; she was, somehow, attracted to grief; while speaking about Misia, during her conversations with Morand, Coco said:

'Other people's grief lures her, just as certain fragrances lure the bee.'

She was one of those people who would arrive at your darkest hour, and that certainly appeared to have been the case with Coco; bringing with her a full party of eclectic personalities and artists; yet both Coco and Morand believed this was not just the result of altruism but because Misia was a dark creature herself, and was attracted to the darkest things in this world.

Misia Sert changed surnames much like hats. By the time she met Coco, she had been married three times already and was living a highly liberal life which clearly caught Coco's attention. Born in 1872, she came from an artistic family, who instilled in her the love for the arts, particularly visual arts, her father whom she adored was a sculptor while her mother had several musical talents. From a very young age, Misia had grown estranged from her father, who much like Coco's was not a devoted figure in her life and had several adulterous relationships. She was sent to live with her grandparents when she was only four, after her mother discovered yet another affair and decided to send Misia and her siblings away. Later, she would join her father and was raised by different stepmothers who would come and go as they pleased from her father's house; she did not develop a relationship with any of them, she felt distant, and somewhat, better, already better than the rest of her family.

It is no surprise that someone like Coco, who had been raised by the infamous, horrible nuns who had turned into aunts in her later childhood recollections, would be drawn to someone like Misia, who'd also had a challenging relationship with her relatives; they had not grown up surrounded by love but both came from a childhood of privations, financial and emotional for Coco, just emotional for Misia.

Misia came from a wealthy family and attended private schools, she grew up in extraordinary wealth and made a name for herself as an acclaimed singer and pianist, with music being her one true love. Her other love or first love came into her life in the shape and form of Thadée Natanson who at the time was the editor of *La Revue Blanche*, a popular magazine covering culture issues of the time.

Inebriated with love and in much need of friends, Misia and her new husband moved to a lovely apartment which was located near to Place de la Concorde and became a low-key editorial office for *La Revue*. That was exactly when Misia became Misia: boasting a strong education and drawing on her privileged background and natural charisma, Misia founded a little group of artists which later became part of Coco's exclusive circle; these people would come to visit her at Place de La Concorde and inspired by her artistry, would paint, make music or write. These personalities of Paris included the likes of Paul Verlaine, Stephané Mallarmé, Toulouse-Lautrec, Auguste Renoir and the Nabis as well as Édouard Vuillard, Pierre Bonard and Felix Vallotton.

People could just join her for the afternoon or stay until late at night, spending time conversing with her, or painting and simply being inspired by Misia, her presence and the beautiful interiors she had so elegantly put together; another thing Coco and Misia shared was a love for styling interiors, something which Coco did several times with her different properties in Paris and everywhere else in the world.

Artists and painters were not the only ones to feel a connection with the Polish pianist, soon, even writers started to populate Misia's world; they would not only write for *La Revue* but also became friends with Misia and often visited her at what was now known in Paris as 'Misia's Salon'. She had become a true authority in Paris, something which she was incredibly proud of, but she became an object of rivalry when Coco, years later, started doing the same thing in Rue Cambon; 'stealing' some of Misia's friends. Some of these famous writer friends included Claude Debussy, Marcel Proust, Apollinaire, Alfred Jarry, Colette as well as Emil Zola, Paul Verlaine and Oscar Wilde. It was an eclectic group of people and Misia quickly became someone highly regarded for the society of the time, the society of the Belle Époque.

While Coco was building herself from scratch, from absolutely nothing, attending events with Balsan, when allowed to do so, and starting to work on her future, Misia was already an acclaimed personality in Paris; her upper-class background had opened many doors for her while her charm had done the rest; she made the most of such a positive, innovative time for French people and with Natanson, she enjoyed a period of joyful calm and creativity. Many artists fell in love with her and she fuelled their inspiration and helped their creative process by offering them help, support and a space to express themselves and their art; she also became a model for many of them, including Renoir and was rumoured to have served as inspiration for Proust' À La Recherche Du Temps Perdu.

Her first marriage didn't last long and after Natanson's financial issues, she started to focus more on her social life; she ended up meeting her future second husband, Alfred Edwards, a millionaire media businessman, during a gala event. When *La Revue* went into administration in 1903, Edwards decided to take his chance, paying off all Natanson's debts and whisking Misia off to Madrid and showering her with gifts and attention. He also bought her an apartment in Rue de Rivoli, which soon became a new pivotal place for the artists of the time, and he married her in 1905.

Misia took back her role as a patron and a socialite in Paris, and threw herself into the creation of a new salon welcoming back old and new friends including a daughter of Marie Curie; she quickly became once again the person to know in Paris, the one connection anyone who was anyone had to make in order to make it.

Even her second husband did not last long and after discovering his affair with Geneviève Lantelme, a theatre personality of the time, Misia, who much like her mother was not forgiving when it came to infidelity, put an end to her marriage to Edwards.

While trying to take a little time for herself and clear out her mind, she managed to meet her third husband and the one she loved the most, Catalan painter, José-Maria Sert. According to different conversations Coco had with Morand, Sert was a good man, larger than life, who enjoyed all the simplest pleasures in life including women and good food; he became a good friend of Coco himself who would call him Jojo affectionately and by whom, she would be called Mademoiselle Chanel in his strong Spanish accent, his musical voice and his passion for food make an appearance more than once in Coco's conversations with Morand.

Coco had made the acquaintance of both Misia and her new husband in her darkest hour, straight after Capel's death; for one reason or another, they had instantly liked each other and the new couple had taken an interest in Coco, in her pain and what she had been going through since Capel's death. It was not an easy time for Coco, she was not her usual productive self and there were days where she could hardly find the motivation to get out of bed or even take care of herself. Jojo Sert and Misia were a perfect antidote to her sadness and depression.

In Coco's conversations with Morand, Jojo Sert was always portrayed as being a full of life, chubby man who was incredibly positive and one of those vibrant souls you rarely encounter in life. He was extremely well-educated and would often share little stories and anecdotes with his friends. In an attempt to fight her own sadness, Coco accompanied Misia and Jojo on an unusual trip to Italy where Sert turned out to be the most perfect tour guide who made it his mission to ensure that they visited and ate pretty much anywhere and everywhere and everything in Rome.

During the day, they walked and walked, marvelling at the beauties of the city while at night, they would stop and eat at the little restaurants where Sert made sure both Coco and Misia tried every single dish.

Sert, in his greatness and immense artistry, was the perfect match for Misia, he was an artist in the true sense of the word, and Misia loved artists. She had grown up with artists and had worked her whole life to keep living between them, being inspired by them, and being one of them. Coco, from her side, was just approaching a more artistically-conscious world, she was a designer yet she knew that in order to become a solid businesswoman in Paris, she had to work strategically and expand her circle of friends; something which had proved necessary now that she had lost Capel, her darling lover, her family and her everything.

Jojo introduced Misia to Sergei Pavlovich Diaghilev, ballet impresario and founder of the Ballets Russes; this established a chain of encounters, connections and projects which later involved Coco as well. Diaghilev told Misia that he wanted to bring the dancers of the Imperial Ballet of Saint Petersburg to Paris for the Spring Season, an ambitious mission and something which had not been done before; Misia, in her endless love for creative people, could not help but fully support the idea and did whatever was in her power to help Diaghilev connect with the right people in Paris as well as enabling him to receive exactly the financial help he needed in order to launch his project. It is exactly there, at that moment, that Misia became the woman she had always wanted to be, the first socialite to grace Paris with her beauty, connections and charisma, and it is there that her patronage first affected the Parisian art scene of the time. While she was busy socialising with the best the French society of the time could offer, she also found herself meeting the one who would become her friend, enemy and inspiration all in one: Coco.

Misia and Coco met one night during a reception organised by actress Cécile Sorel in 1917. They did not like each other instantly and, despite their long-lasting friendship, that instinctive dislike did not leave them; Misia was the first to perceive Coco's genius, her strength and artistic personality; yes, people appreciated Coco's aesthetic sense, her fashion taste and impeccable garments yet it was Misia, the first person, to fully conceive Coco Chanel, the artist. Crushed by the weight of her grief for Capel, Coco easily let the Polish pianist and her world into her life, opening rue Cambon to Misia's friends and starting to follow her everywhere she went. Misia was educated, highly sought within the society of the time and with her help, Coco succeeded in becoming the most superior version of herself, improving her manners and finally embracing a new confidence; something which helped her establish an even more successful business in the first place.

From her side, Coco had quickly become the most innovative fashion designer of the time, someone Misia could not help but feel a little intimidated by. Of course, their friendship was never easy and straightforward, it was challenging yet affectionate. Coco was younger, more beautiful, better dressed and was slowly taking Misia's place in Parisian society; rue Cambon was becoming a new centre for artists, writers and the most highly regarded personalities of the time. Coco was also a little wary of Misia, she didn't entirely trust her as the older woman would often be a little too inquisitive, often asking inappropriate questions about Coco's childhood. As we know by now, Coco worked really hard her whole life to keep her past private almost a secret.

Misia was often called the Queen of Paris and she established relationships with different personalities of the time including Picasso who adored her and painted her portrait several times and Igor Stravinsky who would also later become one of Coco's most famous lovers. It was also Misia who introduced Coco to Diaghilev with the two of them becoming incredibly close friends and financial partners in Diaghilev's new production of the Rites of Spring. Misia and Coco had several things in common: they were both fascinated and loved by artists, and they were particularly involved in the ballet scene of the time as patrons and artists themselves. They could often be found supporting Diaghilev and his productions including the opening of the winter season of Les Biches in Monte Carlo. Monte Carlo represented another important location for both Misia and Coco, in Monte Carlo, Coco met another man who would become an important figure in her life, Britain's richest man Arthur Grosvenor – the Duke of Westminster, or Bendor to his friends.

If Misia had helped Coco during one of the most difficult times of her life, after Capel's death, Coco's designs, fashion and love for anything that was chic and tasteful had a deep impact on Misia and her life; particularly, when after several years of marriage, she discovered Jojo's affair with a half Polish, half Georgian sculptress Roussadanna Mdivani, Roussy to her friends.

At the time, mistresses were not as scandalous and were often quite accepted by the society of the time. Misia turned to Coco for her help, she tried to make herself more appealing in the eyes of Jojo, wore more Chanel, cut her hair but nothing worked; Jojo had fallen in love.

She even tried to include Roussy in her regular family gatherings, inviting her over to dinner and on travels with her and her husband; it didn't bring the result she had hoped and later in 1927, Misia filed for her third divorce.

With the pain of yet another divorce unravelling, it became Coco's job to take care of Misia. She fell ill after finding out that Jojo and Roussy were going to marry shortly after the divorce papers had been signed, and in a miserable attempt to be part of the big celebrations, she helped Roussy choose a wedding dress from Chanel and advised Jojo on the perfect present for his bride. Coco tried to get her to join her in England, thinking that a trip would improve her mood and help her to move forward but Misia chose to join Roussy and Jojo on their honeymoon starting their *ménage trois* all over again. Grief, death and worries brought them closer than ever, they were two friends who would always find each other in time of need and sadness.

When Diaghilev fell ill after years of taking poor care of himself and indulging in alcohol, food and drugs, both Coco and Misia rushed to their friend's side and tried to help him as much as they could, both financially and with the help of their mutual highly sought connections. When news of Diaghilev's deteriorating health reached them, they were once again together, both cruising on the Duke of Westminster's yacht, just along the Dalmatian coast. They rushed to Diaghilev's side; he was their friend and their favourite starving artist. He had been staying in Venice with Sergey Lifar at the Grand Hotel des Bains on the Lido and was not in great shape; it was one of those long, warm summer days yet he was wearing a jacket and could not stop shivering; both Misia and Coco stayed with him until the very end, what else could they do? They were his patrons, his friends and, they would not have done otherwise. While Coco was more accustomed to the idea of death and its lapidary conclusion, Misia did whatever she could to save him, until the very last minute: she called doctors and spent time at his side trying to distract her friend's now delirious mind. Misia and Coco took care of all his bills as well as the funeral and wore white during the service, Diaghilev's favourite colour.

In an attempt to forget a little about the sadness after losing one of their closest friends, Coco and Misa spent some time on Westminster's yacht Flying Cloud, cruising around the Mediterranean as well as spending some time at La Pausa, Chanel's beautiful villa in Roquebrune. La Pausa had become one of the most pivotal centres for artists at the time; and while there, one of her regular guests, film producer Samuel Goldwyn asked Coco to dress some of his most famous film stars.

Misia and Coco, the two friends, embarked on another adventure, they went to the United States and started promoting the Chanel house to the American fashion market, something which deeply affected Coco's fortunes over the following years.

Misia and Coco stayed friends almost until the end, despite going through different ups and downs, Misia was at Coco's side after the loss and the death of yet another lover, French illustrator Paul Iribe, and even pushed her to stand up and work harder against the success and competition of French-Italian designer Elsa Schiaparelli.

Despite their strong intimacy, mutual friends and shared experiences, the two friends lost touch during the Second World War. It is easy to understand the reason behind their separation; Misia and Sert, who had reconciled after Roussy's death, were strongly anti-German while Coco was rumoured to be both an anti-Semite and a Nazi spy because of her relationship with Baron Hans Gunther von Dincklage, and the fact she was allowed to stay at the Ritz during the Paris occupation by German soldiers.

Misia stayed Misia even during the war, helping as many people as she could and when questioned, she still pretended not to know about Coco's whereabouts. In many ways, she kept protecting Coco from a distance, doing something that she was very good at – looking after her friends, those she loved the most, Coco included. Coco grew apart from most of her friends; becoming trapped in rumours, gossip and often lies, quite ironic for someone who had been fabricating stories and had lied about her past for her whole life. Yet her friendship with Misia survived, not even a war could put an end to that. Misia was the annoying sister Coco could not shake off no matter how much she tried, jealous of her yet so protective and always concerned about her wellbeing.

Their friendship was not something Coco would have ever experienced with anyone else; she felt safe with Misia, their relationship was intimate, strong; they had the kind of bond that cannot be broken by disagreement, distance or gossip.

They did lose touch and would hardly speak or meet after the war even after Coco's name was cleared of any relationship with the Nazi; even after she returned to Paris after her self-exile.

The time for parties and artists and passionate affairs had officially come to an end and years later, in the 1950s, Coco met her Polish friend again. Misia had not been well, she had caught a cold, the flu perhaps, something that had forced her to her bed for several days. She must have known, in her profound wisdom, that the end was near; the morning before her death, she made sure to tell her maid that she would have much preferred a Polish service for her funeral. She died shortly afterwards in her sleep. It does not take much to understand Coco's feelings after being informed of Misia's death, the woman who had been by her side throughout her most tragic moments was now gone; she had been lonely for quite some time yet she must have felt like an important chapter of her life, the chapter of beauty and youth perhaps, had finally come to an end; she had no one else to turn to.

She felt it was her responsibility to take care of Misia, one last time.

Demanding as she was, she made sure everything was perfect. She took full charge of her funeral from flower arrangements to personally taking care of Misia's hair, makeup and jewellery for the day which she carefully picked herself. She even arrived to dress her personally in white, a homage to Diaghilev filling her room with just as many white flowers; that was the last time she took care of her old friend, the Queen of Paris was gone.

Coco and Picasso

There is a picture of Coco Chanel and Pablo Picasso, they are both sitting down, both looking at the camera. Fairly young, Coco looks like she is in her late twenties, Picasso is much older. Coco, chic and elegant, is wearing, no doubt, one of her black and white dresses, while also sporting a big black hat. Picasso is in working clothes, but it looks like they are both in Picasso's studio; it feels like the artist has just taken a break from painting.

What did the Spanish painter and the most acclaimed fashion designer have in common? During her conversations with Morand, Coco said that Misia had once claimed that she had protected her from Picasso; she doesn't indulge in the details, but we can understand what she meant. Misia who had been romantically involved with many strong personalities of the time, had also been the lover of Pablo Picasso, a well-known ladies-man who would leave a trail of equally famous lovers behind him; as Misia knew all too well, Picasso had also fallen in love with Coco, but her best friend had done everything in her power to stop the infatuation from its very beginning.

Rumour has it that Coco and Picasso, struck up a relationship anyway, nothing as passionate or as long as the ones she had experienced with some of her other lovers, but still something strong enough to displease Misia.

The reason for Misia's concern was apparent. Picasso had a contradictory, complicated relationship with women, he was inspired by them, loved them yet he was never faithful to them and was always looking for a muse capable of inspiring him a little bit more; she was worried for her friend, still desperate following the tragedy of her Boy.

He was also rumoured to be abusive towards women and often had more than one relationship at the time. He was a sensual man, someone who would often find in his sexuality the medium to inspire his art. He had several interesting personalities of the time as his lovers and married twice.

One of his very first lovers was Laure Germaine Gargallo Pichot, a model and originally the girlfriend of one of his Catalan friends, Carlos Casagemos. The two became closer after Casagemos' suicide but did not stay together long as in 1906 Laure married another friend of Picasso's, Ramon Pichot. Another of Misia's concerns was that often Picasso's women would be stricken by tragedy; that certainly became the case for another woman, Madeleine. There are not many details regarding Madeleine's origin or background or, let alone, what happened to her after her relationship with Picasso; we know that she had an abortion after getting pregnant with his child and broke up with him shortly afterwards. Madeleine, the muse of the cubist painter, also appeared in some of Picasso's most melancholic works, during this time Picasso would often paint mothers with children as if to remember Madeleine and their child together. Picasso would also paint Madeleine during his *Blue Period*, in his works, *Woman in a Chemise, Madeleine Crouching, Woman with a Helmet of Hair, Portrait of Madeleine* and *Mother and Child*.

Picasso had a careless attitude to women and love, he was the cliché of any starving artist, women were his muse, but he was not going to be chained to any of them; this is probably why Misia, who was always half jealous, half protective of all her friends, decided to do something and stop his dangerous interest for Coco.

In the autumn of 1904, Picasso met the love of his life, Fernande Olivier; a French artist and model who had the merit of inspiring both Picasso's *Rose Period* works as well as his very first examples of cubist paintings and sculpture. His relationship with Fernande was wild and complicated, it lasted seven years and culminated in her writing personal memoirs of their life together. It is rumoured that Picasso paid her to stop any further release until his death. A well-known ladies' man, Picasso fell in love with Eva Gouel while still being in a relationship with Fernande; she is the one portrayed in his painting *Woman with a Guitar.* Their relationship didn't last long as Eva died of tuberculosis in 1915.

Whilst in a relationship with Eva, Picasso started to meet with Gaby Depeyre, she was a singer, a dancer and a full-time artist. Picasso could not help himself and although he cared for Eva, he fell in love with Gaby and the two maintained their relationship a secret. Gaby was often found dancing and performing in different cafes in Paris and that is how she got the name of Gaby la Catalane. Picasso and Gaby spent time in the South of France but eventually, Gaby went on to marry Lespinasse, an American businessman who spent several months a year in the South of France. Much like most of Picasso's lovers, Gaby must have known that Picasso was not the man for her; many biographers believe that Picasso proposed to Gaby but that she refused. Picasso was not a man to be trusted and Coco knew that; she had her fair experience with men and she knew that she was better off without them, at least for the time being; Balsan, Capel and all the others had been unfaithful to her, she was not going to go through that again, and that is why later in her conversations with Morand, she would almost mock Misia's interest, dismissing it as Misia being her usual overprotective, inappropriate self. It had not been Misia protecting Coco but more Coco protecting herself.

Coco remembered how jealous Sert, Misia's third husband, was of Picasso, how he had felt that his best years as a painter, as an artist, were behind him and yet Picasso was moving past anything any artist had ever learnt from the masters of the past and was developing a new way to express himself through art. Coco had attended the premiere of Parade, a theatre piece which had been graced with Picasso's sets and costumes. It was something new for the artist, he was a painter and before landing in the French capital, had not thought of any other way to express his talent; yet, as usual, Paris offered him the chance to make connections and take a leap of faith; he was a creative person surrounded by fellow creative personalities and decided to explore what the theatre, the showbiz of the time had to offer someone like him. It was 1917 and

Picasso had joined a group of European avant-garde artists who had grouped together under the direction and vision of Jean Cocteau; this fascinating set included Erik Satie, Pablo Picasso, and Sergei Diaghilev's dance company, the Ballets Russes.

Avant-garde art was often used to describe the French art of the first part of the nineteenth century; in English, avant-garde meant advance guard which stood for that part of an army that moves forward before the rest. Established by philosopher Henri de Saint-Simon, the avant-guard movement encompassed anything that was innovative and defied social norms in both the visual art world as well as literature or any other form of art. Saint-Simon was a socialist and he believed that artists should lead society together with both scientists and industrialists. He strongly believed that art should always have a positive influence and impact. Originally avant-garde art was established by the French painter Gustave Courbet who was highly influenced by socialist ideas and believed in the positive power of modern art and its way to be always innovative, original and almost futuristic.

Picasso's Parade was a dream-infused production which culminated in some incredibly innovative sound-effect as requested by director Cocteau; the sound effect was something new and not completely appreciated at the time; this addition did not make French composer Satie, who was dealing with the production music too enthusiastic, about it. This was also the first time, Satie and Picasso would work together establishing a long-lasting, prolific collaboration throughout their life.

The plot of the Parade was quite engaging as it told the story of a troupe of performers which try to persuade people, passing by, to come and see their show; the troupe itself was a carnival of performers and included a Chinese magician, a young American girl, a pair of acrobats, a horse, and dancers; Picasso who had been the one in charge of costumes had created huge cardboard cubism-inspired outfits which made any movement on stage incredibly difficult, artists could hardly move but it kind of added more to their performance. Picasso was also responsible for the set designs and much like other painters before him including

Salvador Dali, Marc Chagall, André Derain, Joan Miro, and Léon Bakst, had done an excellent job with his sets. However, the production itself became the centre of rumours and scandals causing riots and Erik Satie being slapped in the face by a disappointed spectator. Picasso was the only one who would come out of his first ballet production with dignity and the approval of the society of the time; he would also later marry Olga Khokhlova, one of the dancers of the production. Olga and Picasso were one of the most socialite couples of the time, entertaining friends in their highly fashionable house and indulging in the most glamorous life of clothes, caviar and champagne; they also had a son Paulo who featured in several portraits by Picasso.

It was in this confusing yet entertaining mood that Coco Chanel saw and met Picasso for the first time; they were both in the same circle, attending the same events and Coco's collaboration with the Ballet Russes would have brought them even closer.

Picasso would then go to work for two more productions including Le Tricorne and Pulcinella making his name as both an artist and a theatre designer.

When they met, Picasso had just returned from Rome with Jean Cocteau and Erik Satie and was now exploring what Paris had to offer him, his French was not the best and he shared a flat with poet Max Jacob who taught him the language, especially at first, when no one really knew them yet, they would both lead the artist life, in poverty, with not much food. Coco, who was always drawn to starving artists, was equally drawn to Picasso and the two became friends.

Coco was not a fan of modern art, she was a simple girl who had made simplicity her success: black and white, delicate clothes and no frills involved, she could not fully understand the Spanish painter and his modernism, cubism influences; yet she strongly believed in the power of talented artists and she could see that talent in Picasso.

Pablo Picasso was born in Malaga in Spain in 1811. His father, Don Jose Ruiz y Blasco, was a painter who had seen great potential in his son from the very beginning. He began training with his father and much like other artists before and then, after him, he started by copying the work of other people as well as drawing the human form by looking at live-figure models. When his family moved to Barcelona, his father persuaded the School of Fine Arts to admit him as a student; he was a prodigy and he joined at the age of 13. Later in his life, he would refuse any art school and start painting on his own spending time inside Madrid's Prado.

Much like Coco, his early life was not short of tragedy with his own younger sister dying prematurely of diphtheria, a fatal infection, in 1895.

Picasso's work was so complex that it has been divided by periods of times. He was the co-founder of cubism together with fellow painter Georges Braque. An avant-garde art movement, Cubism had a deep impact on the visual art world as well as music and literature; in Cubism paintings or works of art, objects or subjects are usually broken up into different pieces and redesigned in a new abstract form.

One of his friends and fellow Cubism member, French painter Marie Laurencin, managed to capture Coco in a more abstract form. She painted her in her famous, *Portrait of Mademoiselle Chanel* in 1923. Laurencin was working for Diaghilev's famous Ballet Russes as the costume and set designer for the production of *Les Biches*. That is when she met Coco Chanel who was at the time creating the costumes for the same company's *Le Train Bleu*. In the painting, Coco is portrayed in blue, pink and green with different pets including a white poodle, another dog and a turtle dove. Coco did not like the painting, considering it way too abstract for her tastes, and refused to buy it.

Coco Chanel and Cocteau

There were not many friendships like the one between Coco Chanel and Jean Cocteau; they both shared a strong bond based on mutual adoration and admiration, proof can be found in the several letters exchanged by the two and also in the photographs of the time. Coco was always a little shy when it came to expressing herself artistically, it was a lack of confidence which stayed with her until the very end, yet Cocteau managed to get her to fully exhibit her talent both as a designer and an artist.

Jean Cocteau was born in 1889 near Paris, he was a French poet, a film director, a painter and one of the most influential characters of his time. He was a friend of Coco Chanel and together with her, Picasso and their other friends, he would shape the art and culture of the French society. He considered himself a Parisian, his family belonged to the Parisian bourgeoise and raised him in the appreciation and love of any form of art including literature, painting and music. At the age of 19, he published his first volume of poems, *La Lampe d'Aladin* (*Aladdin's Lamp*). Some of his most important works include several poems, plays and novels like *Les Enfants Terribles* and *La Machine Infernale*. As a director, Cocteau also expanded in the surrealism with motion pictures *Le Sang d'un Poète* and *La Belle et La Bete*.

Jean Cocteau was a troubled, fascinating soul; he spent his life like a true artist writing, creating and spending time with his dearest friends and some of the closest personalities of the time. While spending some time in Chantilly, at the Hôtel du Grand-Condé, he found the inspiration he needed to write *Le Diable au Corps.* (Devil in the Flesh). It was 1923 and that was a pivotal moment for his writing career that led Cocteau to release several works including *Plein-chant, la Rose de François, Le Grand écart* (*The Great Divide*), and *Thomas l'Imposteur* (*Thomas the Impostor*).

At the time, Cocteau was in a relationship with a fellow French poet and writer Raymond Radiguet, a close friend of Mademoiselle Chanel as well. In 1923, Radiguet who had stayed in the Hotel Foyot, died of typhoid. A distraught Cocteau did not even have the strength to attend the funeral; not quite himself after the death of his lover, an upset Cocteau was pushed by some of his close friends, including Diaghilev, Georges Auric and Francis Poulenc to seek a little peace in drugs, including opium.

He started to work more and more for the theatre supporting Coco and the rest of his friends in the production of *Le Train Bleu*. He also started to work on the production for *Romeo & Juliet* which opened at the Théâtre de la Cigale; in the production, he did not only direct the play but also played the role of Mercutio; Maurice Sachs, another writer, also featured in the cast.

Cocteau and his friends, Chanel, Picasso, attended the premiere of *Le Train Bleu* in Paris and one of its performances in London.

The following years were incredibly chaotic for Cocteau who worked with Picasso, he even launched a collection of drawings inspired by the Catalan painter, and succumbed to the ennui with his other friends, finding solace in drugs. At this time, he was still in pain for the death of Radiguet and decided to go to the Maritains with the French composer Georges Auric; despite the pain for the loss of his lover, he still managed to find inspiration and while visiting Picasso, he wrote the poem *L'Ange Heurtebise* (*The Angel Heurtbise*).

After meeting Jean Bourgoint and Bourgoint's sister Jeanne, he found the inspiration for the set of the *Enfants Terribles*. By this time, he had become a heavy drug user and had to seek treatment for opium addiction at the Clinique des Thermes Urbains in rue Chateaubriand. After his recovery, he spent most of this time in Villefrance only going to Paris from time to time; that was when he started to write *Oedipus Rex* for Stravinsky which had its debut at the Théâtre des Arts. It is at this time that he struck up a relationship with the writer and poet Jean Desbordes with whom he would spend several summers in Chantilly and then Côte d'Azur.

Madly in love with Desbordes, he spent several months with him at the Hotel Welcome in Villefrance; despite this, he decided to return to Paris, staying in hotels or sleeping at several friends' homes. Coco decided to help him, once again. She moved to the Ritz and left Cocteau her apartment on rue Cambon; that was when he found the inspiration for *Le Live Blanc* (*The White Book*). Inspired by Paris and its radical ideas, Cocteau started to take a political stand in his works and in *The Mystère laïc* (*The Secular Mystery*), he defended painter Giorgio De Chirico after he had been attacked by surrealists.

Cocteau and Coco decided to spend some time together in Villefrance; once again, he checked himself in a clinic in Saint-Cloud to detox himself from the drugs; Coco was so distraught at the news that she covered the costs herself.

Cocteau stayed at Saint-Cloud until Coco stopped the payment, as he was not getting any better and he started to take opium again; after different issues and tensions, he finally decided to take a break from Desbordes.

Cocteau's life was fragmented by criticism and privations with even the dress rehearsal of *La Voix humaine* (*The Human Voice*) at the Comédie-Française provoking a hostile protest. His relationship with drugs also inspired him to write *Opium, journal d'une désintoxication* (*Opium, Diary of a Detoxification*).

After contracting typhoid in 1931, he spent almost two months in a clinic at Villa Blanche but once in Paris, he started taking opium again. In 1932, he also began a brief but intense affair with Russian aristocrat Natalie Paley (the niece of Tsar Alexander III, born in 1905) but left her once again for Desbordes and moved to Saint-Mandrier. Natalie also aborted their child, something which upset Cocteau greatly. In 1933, he left Desbordes once again and went for another detox.

In 1937, Cocteau met boxing champion Al Brown; he was working as a musician in a cabaret. Thanks to Coco's support, he helped Brown detox so as to make him fit for competition again; something which led him to win the title of World Champion in 1938. That year, Cocteau moved in with French actor Jean Marais and together they travelled to Toulon where they stayed with artist Coula Roppa who much like Cocteau was an avid smoker of opium; after a police raid, they were all accused of drug trafficking.

Once back in Paris, Cocteau attended the premiere of *Les Parents Terribles* (*The Storm Within*) which he had written in only eight days; after a fight with the Paris city council, he risked for his opening to be cancelled as the council tried to ban the performance. When the Second World War unravelled, he and Coco stayed together at the Ritz, he also visited Jean Marais who in the meantime had been mobilised and assigned to a unit. After living at the Hotel du Beaujolais for a while, he travelled to Perpignan with Jean Marais. After learning of the death of his friend and artist Marcel Khill, he returned to Paris and decided to detox himself one more time.

Cocteau was an eclectic personality who was strongly influenced by Coco, whom he admired greatly; he was also influenced by Edouard de Max, who was his mentor and supported him and encouraged him to start writing; he worked and collaborated with many personalities of the time including Pablo Picasso, poet Raymond Radiguet, composer Igor Stravinsky, actor Jean Marais, composer Erik Satie and singer Edith Piaf. He gravitated around these people and often in this bohemian circle, he was known as *The Frivolous Prince* (the title of a book he published at only 22). Cocteau also founded the publishing house Editions de la Sirène which published his books; he was not only influenced by his friends but also influenced his friends, with Stravinsky's, Satie's and Les Six, a group of musicians in Montparnasse, who were inspired by Cocteau and his philosophy.

Cocteau and Coco were so close that at some point in their life, before the Second World War, the media began gossiping about the pair being an item and close to marriage, but that was just a rumour because despite being very good friends and spending most of their life together, they were never a couple.

Coco and Churchill

What did a Parisian fashion designer have in common with one of the most famous British politicians of our time? Very little, at first glance.

Coco and Churchill met through The Duke of Westminster and it was one of those perfect moments destined to change Coco's life. Churchill admired Coco, her strength and personality, and he often said that finally, Westminster had found someone who was a great match to his strong personality. He most certainly appreciated Coco's spirit and the fact that she seemed to be so talented.

Churchill, himself, was a man of many talents, a statesman, a writer, an orator and a leader; he was also the man who brought a British victory during the Second World War. Belonging to the Conservative party, Churchill was prime minister between 1940 to 1945 (he was then defeated by his Labour opponent Clement Attlee) and also from

1951 to 1955 when being increasingly unwell, he conducted most of his business from his bed.

Born in 1874, Churchill came from a wealthy family, but he was not a brilliant student and seemed to have a strong fascination with the military world and joined the Royal Cavalry in 1895. Being a man of many interests, he became a soldier as well as a part-time journalist. He was a keen traveller, and visited several countries including South Africa, Cuba, Afghanistan and Egypt.

Elected as a Conservative MP for Oldham in 1900, he switched to the Liberal Party in 1904 and then back to the Conservative party where he served as a Chancellor of the Exchequer from 1924. After the Tories were defeated in 1929, Churchill lost his seat and spent some time away from the political British world while focusing on his writing, especially speeches. Churchill was drawn to Coco like most people and could forgive her anything, he had been good friends with Westminster for years and through him, he had met Coco. Coco, on her side, has often been defined as an anglophile and would remain that until the very end. Churchill was the one rumoured to have helped her when she had been found sympathising with the Nazis and when many believed her to be a Nazi spy. He had been the one to also help Coco's friend, Vera Lombardi. Coco and Churchill were friends until the very end, he was a good connection to have, something that Coco made the most of during the Second World War.

Coco and Beaton

Cecile Beaton was a friend of Coco's and one of her favourite photographers, he was the one who would take photographs of Coco until the very end. In one of his most appreciated photographs of Mademoiselle Chanel, there is a series of remarkable portraits of Coco who by then in advanced age, still beaming at the camera at the top of her famous stairs in rue Cambon; still dressed in black and wearing her iconic white pearls because any other colour would have been too much, and would have damaged the effortless elegance she had been professing her entire life.

An exhibition in Madrid recently celebrated Beaton and his incredible array of works, celebrating fifty years since the photographer's first solo exhibition at the National Portrait Gallery in London, something which had been sponsored by the then director of the National Portrait Gallery, Sir Roy Strong.

Cecil Beaton was a man adored by many of the leading personalities of the time, he had been lucky enough to take the portrait of several actresses and icons of his day including Audrey Hepburn, Maria Callas and naturally, Coco Chanel.

Beaton was born in London in 1904, right in the middle of the Belle Époque; he had been a witty boy with a strong passion for the arts and a delicate soul. His nanny, 'Ninnie', had been the first to notice his incredible talent and had pushed him to explore it even further, she had been the woman behind the genius and the one to urge young Cecil to start taking more and more photographs, especially those of the people he loved, like his mother and sisters. His nanny also taught him how to develop pictures from an old Kodak, which became Beaton's first camera. Cecil had a strong creative sense and was partial to dramatic settings, that was exactly why in those early years, he could be found taking pictures of his mother and sisters while posing for him in elaborate costumes against almost baroque backgrounds.

Destiny intervened for him, the way destiny does, suddenly, without much of a warning and rapidly; it was 1927 and Beaton took a picture of his friend and supporter Stephen Tennant, the two had been friends for many years, and that picture became the manifesto for Bright Young Things. This was a group that boasted many leading lights of the time as its supporters; the group celebrated a certain hedonistic lifestyle and was often the devious mind behind different treasure hunting events in London which were run under the effect of alcohol and drugs. Both Beaton and Tennant were completely drawn to the movement's core values and fully embraced them. Beaton, like many members of the group, was bisexual and went on to have several relationships with high profile men and women, including actress Greta Garbo and Olympic fencer and teacher Kinmont Hoitsma.

During this time, Beaton took several pictures of the Bright Young Things. He had many talents and tried acting when he was younger, but photography was what he excelled at. In the 1930s, he acquired a beautiful mansion in Ashcombe where he would invite guests, mainly members of the Bright Young Things, and take their pictures; the best thing about these weekends away was the eccentricity of Beaton's photography style which urged his guests to dress up and change costumes to please their host.

Beaton soon found fame in New York and was employed by several Conde Nast magazines including *Vogue*, he also went on to take several photographs of the royal family including Queen Elizabeth at Buckingham Palace, her later coronation in 1953 and also the wedding of Princess Margaret and Anthony Armstrong-Jones.

During The Second World War, Beaton made his fortune by becoming employed by the Ministry of Information to take pictures from the home front and in different war zones; his efforts are still today the best photographic collection we have from the war and had a deep impact on the public opinion. One, in particular was especially remembered for its dramatic message, it was a picture of a three-year-old, Eileen Dunne, who had fallen victim of the bombing; that same picture of Eileen and of her teddy bear had the power of persuading America to join the war.

In 1947, Beaton went through a quiet phase in his life, maybe the horror of the war had changed him for good and he could not stand the superficiality of his younger years. He focused on the things he genuinely loved the most including fashion photography and the theatre, he managed to direct sets and costumes for over ten movies and different plays such as *My Fair Lady*. Beaton also worked on creating setting and costumes for the *Coco Chanel* musical with Katharine Hepburn, something which Coco was not exactly thrilled about. Coco believed Katharine to be too old for the role and was not enthusiastic about her or the musical itself. Beaton won three Oscars for both his iconic costumes and art direction for the film versions of *My Fair Lady* in 1965 and for *Gigi* in 1958.

However, it was with Coco, the musical and first representation of Coco and her life that he risked losing his reputation. It was 1969 and *Coco*, the musical, ran for nine and a half months at the Mark Hellinger Theatre. Directed by Michael Benthall and with the choreographies of Michael Bennet as well as the music of Previn, the musical was one of the most expensive Broadway productions of all the time and Beaton himself personally designed over two hundred costumes based on the designs of Coco Chanel.

Coco would have much preferred to design the costumes herself, as she had done several times for other productions, but the musical production decided to go for Beaton. Beaton created a more dramatic version of the Chanel interiors including her apartment and the mirrored staircase. Eventually, Hepburn went to meet Coco and the two seemed to really like each other, Hepburn was in awe of the iconic fashion designer and Coco seemed, despite everything, taken by the actress just as much. According to *Sleep with Enemy's* biographer Hal Vaughan, following their meeting, Hepburn returned to rue Cambon after forgetting something, perhaps her bag, and she found Coco napping on her sofa; she said that it had been only then that she had realised she was, no doubt, the right person to play the infamous French designer, Coco was only human after all.

The reviews for *Coco the Musical* were not the best and Beaton did not come out of the experience looking great, as the press did not sound enthusiastic about his work or the musical itself; Katharine Hepburn was the only one praised by the media for her talent and unexpectedly good voice.

Much like Coco and many influential personalities of the time, Beaton was an anti-Semite and it is rumoured that his ideas cost him his collaboration with *Vogue*. A strong personality and important figure of his time, Beaton died in 1980, previously a stroke had paralysed his right arm and he had taught himself how to write and draw with his left hand.

Coco and Lifar

Serge and Coco were friends for a lifetime. Serge was an international dancer and choreographer and he was also the director of the Paris Opera Ballet, and he created what it is now known as the modern French ballet. Lifar also performed with the Ballet Russes from 1923 to 1929, where he and his good friend Diaghilev inspired each other. Lifar was known for being a fierce character and he once refused to dance because he didn't like the setting. He also challenged opponents to a duel twice in his lifetime. Lifar was an eclectic personality, someone Coco loved dearly, and who was responsible for bringing to light several famous dancer personalities including Yvette Chauvire, Nina Vyroubova, Solange Schwarz and Lycette Darsonval.

Lifar is mostly remembered for his work at the Paris Opera where he served as a ballet master from 1929 to 1945 and then later from 1947 to 1958. Much like Coco, he was accused of collaborating with the Nazis and left Paris in 1945 after being photographed in the company of several German officers. Like Coco, he was cleared of any charge yet several of his works and performances were boycotted by fans as a protest, not many believed him, and the boycott did not stop there. Many people working behind the scenes at some of his ballet productions, 'stagehands' refused to work with him in protest against his apparent involvement with the Nazis during the Second World War. Years later, and only, thanks to the intervention of Georges Hirsch, director of the Paris Opera, and leader of the French resistance, he managed to restore his reputation in New York when Hirsch took to his defence after protests had attempted to shut down Lifar's show. Later, he worked for the Paris Opera on an ad-hoc basis as a choreographer, with his last ballet being choreographed in Lausanne in 1960. Coco and Lifar remained friends until the very last; Coco was devoted to him, he was an eclectic performer, innovative and often eccentric, something which she loved; he was also temperamental and we know that Coco loved to befriend people who reminded her of herself, of her strong, fiery personality. She was an artist who loved artists and Lifar was one of her favourites.

Culture Chanel, in conversation with Gabriella Belli, the director of the Foundation for the Municipal Museums of Venice and scientific curator of Culture Chanel

The Chanel myth was most recently brought back to life by the exhibition curated by artistic director and art critic Jean-Louis Froment collaboration with art historian, curator, and currently director of the Foundation for the Municipal Museums of Venice, Gabriella Belli. It was a touching homage which opened with an exquisite handwritten note by Coco herself which read:

> 'The life we lead always amounts to so little, the life we dream of, that's the great existence because it continues on after our death.'

Coco was an exceptional reader who owned several books in her library and who found in literature the comfort and peace she so desperately needed. It is not wrong to assume that Coco became the heroine of her own life, thanks to the books she read and most importantly, the authors she connected with. Her library offered a bit of everything from antiquity to contemporary fiction and included the works of Sophocles, Virgil, Rabelais, Shakespeare, Montaigne, Madame de Sévigné, Baudelaire, Verlaine, Barbey d'Aurevilly, Lautréamont, Rilke, Proust, Claudel, Apollinaire and Mallarmé.

She was particularly partial to poetry and she nurtured long-lasting friendships with some of the most important poets of her time including Jean Cocteau, Max Jacob and Pierre Reverdy, who ended up dedicating several letters and poems to her.

Here I talked to the scientific curator of Culture Chanel, Gabriella Belli, about the exhibition and what it meant to her to bring to the public this unexpected side of Coco.

Culture Chanel

> 'The exhibition has given ample testimony to the many correspondences Chanel had with her friends who have admired

her creative boldness, determination and strength especially when she had to get back on her feet throughout her life, because although often we consider Coco Chanel today a strong myth, even she had to go through some difficult days. More than a letter, the words that struck me most are those that she wrote in 1932 herself in a manuscript of memoirs: 'all means are legitimate in the profession I practise, as long as the designer never leaves that method that consists in making women even more beautiful ...'

'It is a strong, precise affirmation that reveals in her a real mission, that Coco wanted to be at service to women helping them to bring light to their personalities, letting their beauty, not exclusively physical, shine through.'

'Let each woman wear herself: fashion, therefore, was not only regarded as an instrument of affirmation of a more feminine personality, but also as a liberation from conventions, stereotypes, and the respectable constraints of a society, like the one of her time, that was conservative and not very inclined to recognise her talent and to appreciate her well-declared unconventionality.'

Another Coco...

'It is evident that the vast public that visited the exhibition set up in the halls of the Ca 'Pesaro international modern art gallery was able to get to know another Coco Chanel, unexpected as it was incredibly interesting. All those who entered the door of the exhibition would have expected to see clothes, jewellery, perfumes and instead, they were greeted by an autographed manuscript of a masterpiece of world literature, Madame Bovary by Gustave Flaubert. A prologue that immediately solicited in the public a change of perspective, a bewilderment and at the same time a great curiosity. Coco's like Emma? No, maybe not, but the metaphor was compelling, the boarding school, the discovery of love, the music: hadn't the whole world that revolved around Madame Bovary been in some ways even the one of the very young Coco? It is from this surprising beginning that the exhibition immediately revealed another Chanel, the intimate, reflective, religious one, focused on the urgency of knowing; she almost self-taught, struggling with the reading of the most "high" works of prose and of world poetry, sharing with intellectuals more engaged of her time dreams, passions, loves. From this perspective, no one had ever looked at her work as a queen of high fashion.'

Stravinsky and The Rite of Spring

'The autographed manuscript score of the Rite of Spring by Igor Stravinsky, was the work that struck me most. It's a real gem, and my favourite item from the exhibition. Among Coco Chanel's most intimate friends, Stravinsky occupies a central place in the Paris of the early 1910s, he was a strong personality of the time who was involved in a radical revision of the musical composition tradition. This manuscript with autographed annotations, corrections and amends did not belong to Chanel but that amazing music that brought to life all the energy of forgotten pagan rites of ancient Russia was a source of great inspiration for her imagination, always in search of new suggestions. After all, Stravinsky's close association will give her the friendship of two of her most faithful companions, Misia Sert and Sergei Diaghilev, both Russians, both eccentric and non-conformist just like Coco.'

Coco, her friends, her world

'It is difficult to measure the weight and influence that external factors may have had on the formation of the personality of Coco Chanel and her creativity. But there is no doubt that if by definition creativity is always nourished by everything that surrounds it, and therefore also by readings, friendships, sounds and rhythms of music, lights and colours of painting, this was the case for Chanel as well, eager as she were to know and learn from an early age what the world offered her. Between the Divine Comedy and Madame Bovary there would seem to be a sidereal distance, but not for

Mademoiselle who knew how to cultivate Emma's inspiration and Virgil's severity at the same time. These readings were associated with the evenings and friendship with the most highly regarded Parisian intellectuals of the time, never occasional acquaintances but mostly long acquaintances, who saw amazing fruits growing in the imaginary universe of Coco Chanel; a unique precipitate of loves and passions, of philosophical reflections and moral dissertations, of coup de theatre and metaphysical reveries. Her fashion has grown with the lightness of Apollinaire's verses and the syncopated rhythm of Stravinsky's music, with the sensuality of Nijinsky and the narrowness of wartime, with the unhappiness of lost loves and the desire to win of her indomitable personality.'

In conversation with Jeffie Pike Durham, daughter of Marion Pike, artist and Coco Chanel's friend

She is looking at you, straight at you, but she is not judging. You would expect her to be, after all, she is the icon and she is the style. Maybe it is the comforting blue shades of the background or maybe it is the sweet eyes, one cannot help but wonder if they were that sweet in real life or were in fact donned by someone who must have loved her very much; it is like looking at a direct, loving expression of the painter herself. Yet, it is the depth of the eyes that is mesmerising; they are deep, deeper than any other portrait anyone has ever done of her. Once the attention moves from the eyes to the painting, it is difficult not to feel overwhelmed: the beauty is in the details, details that leave you with a strong impression of what she must have been like in real life. You see beautiful earrings, a blue, red and white scarf, the colours of the French flag to mark her origins, a little blue hat, of course, to remind us all of how it started, and a short Boy haircut, the garçon look, the rebel inside of her; which is still present, still alive.

In this painting of Coco Chanel, Marion Pike, painter, all-around artist and just an incredible woman manages to cut through to Coco's essence and what it is that has made her an icon to transcend time and generations. This picture makes her eternal unlike any other portrait, picture or movie had ever done before. It's an intimate glimpse of Coco's soul, a fragment of her life. She was 84 at the time and had just met Marion who was thirty years younger.

The two women struck up a unique friendship – here I talk with Jeffie Pike Durham about her mother and Coco.

Can you tell me a bit about your mother and her background?

'Born on a family ranch in Mendocino County in 1913, my mother was a third-generation Californian, the niece of the legendary frontiersman and explorer Kit Carson. She always said she was "born with a pith helmet on" ready to set out and see the world. And that is exactly what she did.

By the time she was accepted to Stanford at age 14, she had already been abroad – to Venice and Paris, where, in 1924 at age 12, she saw a Delacroix exhibition at the Louvre that made an unforgettable impression on her. At age 16, she made her second trip to Europe – travelling again with her parents to Paris, Italy, Switzerland, Austria, and Hungary. In 1932, as an Oriental History major at Stanford, she set out for Japan, Korea and China and celebrated her 19th birthday in Beijing.

At home in San Francisco, my mother was brought up in a house, inspired by the Petit Trianon – Marie Antoinette's Chateau in the gardens of Versailles. My mother's mother, Rose, visiting the Petit Trianon on her honeymoon with her second husband, Sam Pauson, told him she'd really like one of those! So, Sam, besotted with his beautiful bride, acquired a full city block, hired an architect who had studied at the Ecole des Beaux Arts in Paris, and built Rose her very own Trianon on Jackson Street. Filled with treasures both French and Asian, it could have been decorated by Coco Chanel herself.

Even though my mother's taste was modern – Frank Lloyd Wright designed a house and studio for her– I often wondered if going to dinner at Coco's was like going home again. Sitting in Coco's dining room in her private quarters above the atelier on Rue Cambon, I thought that my mother looked like a contented child, once again at Rose's table.

My mother's wardrobe, carefully selected by Rose, could also have been chosen by Chanel. In 1927, riding her horse in San Francisco's Golden Gate Park, my mother was attired in a riding habit – perfectly tailored mannish jacket with jodhpurs and high soft leather boots – an outfit strikingly similar to the one Coco Chanel was photographed wearing in Scotland with the Bendor, the Duke of Westminster, and Winston Churchill. My mother, age 14, and Coco, age 44, would not meet for another 40 years but they already had the same appreciation of style and quality.

Even though my mother was outfitted in the most elegant formal riding habit – black for competition- and gifted with the most magnificent 5-gaited horse, Blanche McDonald, she was also told that if she ever failed to place first in competition and bring home the blue ribbon or silver cup, her horse would be taken away from her. Luckily for my mother, she was always able to win. Years later, those silver trophies filled with my mother's paint brushes were dotted around her studio – but without much fanfare, comment or attention. If you asked my mother what they were or how she got them, she'd just shrug and say, "Oh well, that was a long time ago."

And it was. A lifelong workaholic who never thought she knew enough or was good enough, my mother did not dwell on her past. Still, we all knew, from her many friends, that she, Marion Hewlett, graduated from college in 1933 with a frontpage headline in the Stanford Daily: Hewie Leaves, Stanford Mourns." To us, she was still the same exuberant, fun-loving character she'd been on campus. It took only a little prompting to get her to jump up and start the Stanford cheer, "Give 'em the ax, the ax, the ax, harder, harder…!" We'd laugh, she'd laugh, and then with a little skip or dance, she'd go back to her easel. But she was also a serious scholar who never stopped acquiring art books which she studied every day of her life, and a stack upon stacks of non-fiction books – memoirs, history, philosophy – which she read until the early morning hours, often falling asleep reading.

Because of an old red blanket folded and stored in the back of the linen closet, we also found out that she was one of the first women to win the Stanford Block S Blanket for sports – a feat accomplished by being on fourteen first teams. She played golf with the men because she needed some competition and the women couldn't drive the ball as far as she could – a stand not unlike the one Coco took when she refused to ride side-saddle like a lady. Instead, Coco put on pants so she could straddle a horse too wild for anyone else to handle, take off through the trees and give everyone a good show.

What did it take to be a great equestrienne or a great golfer – especially if you were, like both my mother and Coco, of slight, small stature? Neither of them was more than 5′ 3″ tall. The answer, in addition to balance and coordination, is great hands. Both my mother and Coco had those hands and created with those hands. Coco used her hands to work directly with her materials, both the fabrics she would drape over the body – scissors, pins and needles in hand – or the masses of chains she would rifle through in search of just the right one. My mother always said that she felt the urge to create in her hands – it wasn't in her head but in her hands that she would itch to pick up a paint brush and go to work.

After Stanford, instead of becoming a professional golfer, the next Babe Didrikson as suggested in local newspaper articles, my mother decided to take art more art classes – in San Francisco and Carmel. Two decades later, in 1955, after a one-woman retrospective at San Francisco's California Palace of the Legion of Honor, she returned to Paris and to the museum that had first captured her 12-year-old attention: The Louvre. Instead of resting on her laurels – believing the reviews by critics who pronounced her a talented and mature artist – she fled the art scene in the United States, obtained a permit to copy the masterpieces hanging at the Louvre, and happily resumed her preferred status: student. She was 42 years old.

From that moment, until her death at age 84, my mother never stopped working. Whether she travelled to paint the Pope in Rome, symphony conductor Zubin Mehta rehearsing the Los Angeles Philharmonic, pianist Artur Rubinstein dictating his memoirs in Marbella, film and Broadway star Roz Russell at home in Los Angeles, Coco Chanel designing her collection in Paris, Louise de Vilmorin reading at her chateau outside of Paris, the rocky hills of Corsica, the skies off Claudette Colbert's beach in Barbados, the volcano across the lake from her Atitlan house in Guatemala, the green fields surrounding her barn-turned-studio in the Sologne, Prime Minister Lee Kwan Yew in Singapore, Metropolitan opera star Licia Albanese in New York, Lucille and Norton Simon in

Los Angeles or Ronald and Nancy Reagan at the White House, she was always on the go. Always off to study – Rembrandt in Amsterdam, Piero Della Francesca in Italy, Goya in Madrid – she never stopped trying to learn a little more, trying to understand what made great works of art stand the test of time, trying to become a better and better painter.

The energy she had as a child – a surging, competitive, irrepressible energy that by her own admission "exhausted everyone" around her – was the driving force behind a body of work that spanned three continents and seven decades.'

Why was your mother in Paris at the time?

'My mother was in Paris in the 1960s because she had decided when I went to college in 1958 to live there part-time. For her, there was nothing like the Paris light – the Seine, the Paris rooftops. Just being there inspired her to paint. She also persuaded a farmer to allow her to renovate one of his barns in the Sologne where she loved painting fields, trees and wildflowers.

My mother also had a very interesting circle of French friends who made her feel that she belonged.

Two close friends were Andre Malraux, author, art expert, de Gaulle's Minister of Cultural Affairs, and Louise de Vilmorin, novelist, poet and journalist who lived at her family Château Verrières-le-Buisson. Louise offered my mother a studio there, but when turned down simply gave my mother a standing invitation to her famous Sunday suppers.

Those gatherings were ones my mother never wanted to miss, for she said that the guests were always intelligent, sometimes brilliant, and she always learned something. Malraux, when he was in residence, would regale the table with tales that were riveting and amusing – discussing everything from the lost kingdom of the Queen of Sheba to Sassanian belt buckles. My mother said he was the most fascinating man she ever met.

Louise and Malraux were the only two people Jackie Kennedy requested to see when she and President Kennedy went to Paris. Afterwards, Malraux and Jackie took the Mona Lisa to the Metropolitan Museum in New York for a special viewing which caused long lines around the block.

Louise was also a friendly enemy of Chanel. The key point here is the tolerance Louise and Coco had for my mother's friendship with both of them. Neither objected, which speaks volumes about the independence my mother enjoyed. Both Coco and Louise saw my mother's talent and asked her to paint their portraits.

Another special friend was Madeleine "Mado" Hours, the Conservator at the Louvre, who stopped on her daily rounds to watch my mother attempt to capture the brush strokes and light in the Rembrandt self-portrait. Studying Rembrandt was my mother's sole reason for returning year after year and activating her permit to "copy" at the Louvre. Eventually, Mado introduced herself and slowly, as my mother continued to work, befriended her. Perhaps because my mother was working in the time-honoured tradition of copyist or student the way such greats as Renoir, Degas and Manet had Mado decided to introduce my mother to Julie Manet Rouart, the daughter of artist Berthe Morisot and Eugene Manet, and her first cousin, Jeannie Gobillard Valery, wife of the great French poet Paul Valery.

When Julie's parents both died and left her an orphan at age 16, she went to live with her cousins and she and Jeannie became best friends. They were married together in a double ceremony in 1900. Both of their husbands, Ernest Rouart and Paul Valery, died in the 1940s.

The two elderly widows felt an immediate connection with my mother and agreed to sit for their portraits. They were full of stories and loved to gossip – so my mother was treated to many lively personal tales about family friend Renoir, Julie's Godfather Degas, and Julie's uncle, Edouard Manet. As Julie and Jeannie had posed for all of them, in addition to posing for Julie's mother

Berthe Morisot, their willingness to sit for a portrait by my mother was certainly an honour.

I was lucky enough to pay a visit to Mme Rouart in 1963. She lived in the top floor apartment of the house her mother Berthe Morisot had built on the Rue Paul Valery (street renamed in his honour when he died in 1946). At age 84, Julie Manet Rouart was tiny, stood ramrod straight and wore a dress that buttoned from head to toe. When she opened the door on the dark corridor, a flood of bright sunlight greeted us and illuminated a wall of paintings hung in tiers – each one more amazing than the other. She had so many paintings, they were everywhere, leaning against the backs of chairs, stuffed into closets – all gifts, a private collection of masterpieces.

Between 1966 and 1967, my mother was still putting the finishing touches on her double portrait of the cousins, Mesdames Rouart and Valery, and she had just started a portrait of Isabelle, the Countess of Paris. Commissions such as these and plans to travel were on her calendar when one of her old friends from California arrived in Paris and asked her to make time to meet Coco Chanel.'

How did your mother meet Coco?

'In 1967, after lobbying for a decade, Roz Russell's husband, Freddie Brisson, persuaded Chanel to let him produce a Broadway musical based on her life. The title: Coco. As a producer, Freddie's challenge was to bring many new people together to work on the show – Americans at the forefront. Perhaps because my mother had done several portraits of Roz and Roz had loved the process, Freddie thought that Coco would respond the same way and be happy to meet even more Americans who would need to get to know her as they created the show.

Freddie's problem was that Coco said she had no interest in meeting an American painter, and my mother's schedule was jam-packed. My mother had nothing against Chanel. She liked Chanel clothing – in fact, she had recently bought an evening ensemble and had also acquired the same pink suit Jackie Kennedy wore to Texas – but she told Freddie she just didn't have time. Maybe she could do it at a later date.

Fortunately, Freddie was persistent. He apparently thought that it would help him if Chanel were to meet my mother before he brought in Katharine Hepburn, Alan Jay Lerner and André Previn. We'll never know how he did it, but Freddie called my mother in a great rush to announce Coco's invitation and to beg my mother to go to 31 Rue Cambon the following day at 3:00 PM. Freddie told my mother that she never had to go back but would she please show up the next day – as a favour to him? My mother said she would.

When my mother arrived, Coco was busy doing a fitting on a model and continued to do so for about an hour. My mother, fascinated by the scene with all the assistants and bolts of cloth and Coco's complete absorption in her task, simply leaned against the wall and sketched. Then, suddenly, Coco took a break, walked over to my mother, and asked to see her sketch pad. After flipping through it, she said, "You have the hand of a real artist!" Then, taking off a scarf she was wearing, Coco put it around my mother's neck and said, "Here is a souvenir of our first meeting. I know we are going to become friends. Could you please come back tomorrow?"

Within three days of that meeting, Coco had invited my mother to set up her easel and work on-site, any time she liked, right in the atelier while Coco was doing her fittings. Soon, as they worked side-by-side, the easel was replaced by scaffolding for the enormous works my mother would create (Chanel in her Atelier, Diptych 255 × 300 cm; Chanel – Big Head 246 × 150 cm) and Coco herself got into the act. After my mother left for the day, Coco liked to climb up and fix the shoulder or make the cuffs on the shirt whiter. Coco loved to say that my mother was a great enough artist not to mind, and my mother would laugh – usually explaining that to create a brilliant, bright white, a painter juxtaposes several shades which mix in the mind's eye. Coco must have known that, but she was having the time of her life – participating, joking, and feeling rejuvenated by this new collaboration and friendship.

Their bond lasted for the rest of their lives, for it was based on complete respect and total admiration for one another's artistry. Coco told one reporter that she couldn't have done her 1968 collection without my mother, for my mother was a genius who inspired her. My mother, I believe, was the daughter Coco herself would have designed if she'd been asked to ...'

What's your favourite memory of Coco?

'My memory is a kaleidoscope:

My first "take" on the slight, wiry figure perched on the edge of a luxurious expanse of faun colored suede couch: there she was, elegant and worldly, then in the blink of an eye, an old crone with a necklace of bird feathers, teeth and shells around her neck – someone with the power to look right through you and beyond. Each time I saw her, Chanel had that dual persona – a fashion icon in rich jewels and an ancient seer wearing magic talismans.

Then, our goodbye: one afternoon Coco took me aside, patted the suede cushion and asked me to sit right there, next to her on the couch, the only time I was invited to do so. In a low voice, she said I must pay attention and always remember what she was about to tell me, which was this: "In years to come, no one will remember me or my clothes. I'm just a little dressmaker. But your mother is a great artist. She is the one who will be known by future generations. Yes – her work will last for all time."

Finally, the little bird: it was the Winter of 1998 and my mother was 84, the same age Coco was when they met. I had just taken my mother her café au lait in bed, when out of the blue she started talking about Coco who had died twenty-seven years before in January 1971. My mother said, "One day when Coco sensed that the end was near, she took my face in her hands and told me to wait and watch for a little bird, for it would carry a message that she was fine and just waiting for me to join her. In the Spring, maybe two months after Coco died, a little bird came and sat on the planter box outside of my window in Paris. It cocked its head and seemed to be trying to tell me something. All of a sudden, I knew it was Coco, paying me a visit, just the way she said she would." My mother died a week later, February 4, 1998. Did my mother really believe that she'd had a visitation from Coco? So, it would seem.'

Chapter 9

Coco, the Only One

At first, Coco's main competitors were women such as Lanvin, and Schiaparelli. But later, her business rivals were also men; and her competitors who didn't sketch and did not work directly on the body with the precision that she did were one of her motives for staging a comeback in 1953. She wanted the world to know that she, Chanel, was more than just a fragrance. Coco Chanel was back and ready to give women what they didn't even know they needed or wanted.

Becoming an icon like Coco Chanel had not been an easy task. Yes, she was loved, admired and sometimes feared but maintaining her status, her business and her reputation was not an easy job. She had to do everything in her power to keep producing great ideas for her collections, yet she was also a businesswoman, and she had to take care of herself and her business too. A few things did not go as planned, first, she found herself in the middle of several strikes as her workers demanded fairer, better working conditions, paid holidays, and pay rises. Coco was not ready to give in to any of these demands, but in 1936, when the French socialist Leon Blum became the prime minister of France, he made fairer working conditions mandatory for workers. It was a vague, uncertain time for the wealthy and powerful people of Paris; as the workers were not ready to compromise anymore, they wanted better conditions, their work mattered, they knew they were the powerful force behind the tireless machines that the clothing industry or any other industry was. They also knew that there was not going to be any production, any fashion system and any Chanel without them; that gave them the motivation they needed to start a number of powerful strikes to make their voices heard.

One morning, Coco herself and her faithful accountant were banned from entering the Chanel boutique and offices, with Coco's salesgirls and seamstresses effectively occupying the Chanel house. The trouble was that Coco did not expect such betrayal from her 'girls', she was mostly a good employer and she gave them a decent wage for their work. She did not come from money herself and so she knew what it was like to work for others; and she could not help but feel betrayed by her workers. Yet, it was far from being personal, strikes had been taking place everywhere in Paris, from Printemps to Lafayette; workers were finally learning to recognise their importance, and how much they mattered, and Chanel's girls were caught up in that sudden sense of power.

The settlement did not come from Coco but from Blum who managed to sign an agreement with the French labour movement, which meant that workers would only be allowed to work for forty hours a week. They would also be granted paid holiday and it became mandatory for everyone to attend school until the age of 14.

Coco was not happy about any of this, she would work herself silly every day and would expect the same from her collaborators, the idea of having to pay holiday was also equally inconceivable to her, she was not ready to give up on her principles; it did take some convincing and in the end, she accepted the new conditions in the name of her business. She had made investments and quite reluctantly, she had to admit she needed the workforce.

Another issue was her success in the United States which made her less popular in France. Coco had become an international designer, and many thought she had sold her soul to the almighty dollar, believing she would do whatever it took for fame and success. In America, she had started to dress the stars, making costumes for movies; she dressed Hollywood actress Gloria Swanson in the movie *Tonight or Never*, and also Madge Evans, Ina Claire and Joan Blonder in the 1932 film, *The Greeks Had a Word for Them*. Her trip to the US was short and did not bring her the success she had hoped for. Yes, she had gained publicity and fame, she had been put on the international US fashion map and had made money, yet she was not being feted by the fashion world as much as she had hoped. It was not an easy time for Coco, and it was made particularly hard by the fact new designers were just coming out of nowhere all the time and she felt she could hardly keep up.

Coco and Schiaparelli

Back in Paris, Coco was going through a lot. She had lost the loyalty of her workers, she was still bitter about her first lukewarm American experience and she also had to face one of her worst fears; while she had been gone, trying to find her fortune in America, fashion designer Elsa Schiaparelli had slowly replaced her in the Parisian fashion world. However, something that Coco could not realise at the time was that Elsa Schiaparelli, was her perfect match – someone who could only motivate her to do better and, to always, strive for success.

Italian-born Elsa Schiaparelli was a fashion designer who had been educated in Paris; after finishing her education in France, Britain and Italy, Elsa managed to successfully establish an important couture house in Paris. She was a fashion designer and made sure everyone knew about that, not a hat-maker like Coco, she would stress. Her relationship with Coco was always difficult, the two were competitors, rivals and would thrive off each other's creative genius. Elsa was famous for her original, innovative fashion, she was inspired by surrealism in all her creations which culminated in the design of some incredibly smart accessories such as telephone-shaped purses. Much like Coco, Schiaparelli was an independent woman with an even stronger personality. She came from an upper-class family, but she had run away quite young to go and work as a translator in the United States. In the 1920s, she finally settled in Paris where Coco had already made a name for herself and by becoming one of the most sought-after and admired designers, she started to expand her range of couture dresses by adding jewellery, perfumes, cosmetics, lingerie and swimsuits.

If Coco was always simple, elegant, measured in all her creations and had made the perfectly fitted outfit, her signature look, Schiaparelli offered an alternative to Coco's minimalism, creating eccentric yet innovative and original outfits which were still highly wearable. In 1947, she was the first designer to use shocking pink for the first time, pushing women to be a little braver when it came to using colour; something that was extremely well-received especially after the horrors of the Second World War as women had certainly had enough of wearing black. Pink became a colour for feminism, something which perfectly suited what women stood for. Schiaparelli, who had moved to New York during the Second World War, began to mass-produce her dresses in 1949 with the launch of a new collection.

Coco and Schiaparelli would never become friends, Coco called her 'L'italianne' while Schiaparelli would call her 'the hatmaker'. Schiaparelli worked with some of Coco's closest friends including Cocteau, she also collaborated with Dali, using the pink from his palette as well as being inspired by the works of art of Christian Berard. Many famous people loved her creations, including American socialite Wallis Simpson and Anita Loos, a famous playwright, and the author of *Gentlemen Prefer Blondes*. Schiaparelli was a breath of fresh air, as she would use new materials which reassembled plastic and would attract the interest of fashion customers; she also designed a skirt with pockets with flaps that took the shape of lips. It was not an easy time for Coco, and like many romantic heroines, she had found a rival, a competitor, someone who could replace her in the hearts of Parisian women, someone who was an innovator and embraced new trends, something that Coco never did.

Coco and Dior

It was probably Christian Dior who managed to drag Coco back to Paris, out of early retirement in 1953. It was him and the new world of possibilities he and other designers were starting to offer to French women that ignited the fashion fire in her belly. She was not dead yet, and she could still teach a thing or two to these new designers.

She strongly believed that fashion designers, like Dior, did not care much about women and what they liked; Coco did not understand the need for the extra feminine clothes or for the delicate, flowery designs. In many ways, she must have seen it as a defeat, she had worked her entire life, trying to give women the direction she thought was right, clothes that were as practical as men's. She had been the woman to make dresses suited and more accessible and to remove the extra feathers. So, she had a real problem accepting new designers who celebrated a more traditionally feminine look.

There she was, self-exiled in Switzerland, while these designers were dictating new fashion rules, she had to make her voice heard and so she came out of retirement and started fighting back, for women and for her strong sense of pride, something she had never left behind. She was under the impression that these new designers, were not there to satisfy women but to feed their very own egos with eccentric looks and excessive accessories.

Christian Dior was a French fashion designer who had made his fortune after the Second World War, making his name just as Coco's reputation was being tainted by the Nazi rumours and her alleged anti-Semitic views. His take on fashion became popular at a time when women wanted to erase the horrors of the war.

Dior was born in Northern France in 1905, he was younger than Coco and had been admiring her work from a distance. But he saw women differently to Coco, and he had the strong urge to give them a little break, a little luxury after all the suffering of the Second World War. He worked hard to reintroduce a more feminine fashion which focused on luxury fabrics. His designs were popular with his customers who particularly liked the innovation behind them, an innovation which Coco often found exaggerated, but nevertheless, Dior sealed the approval of the best actresses of the time as well as the Royal family.

Born in Granville, Dior was the second of five children and the son of a fertiliser manufacturer whose tremendous success gave Christian the start he needed in his life; he moved to Paris with his family when he was only a boy and soon, he started to manifest a strong passion for the arts, especially anything related to visual art, he would sketch all day and seemed to have a strong interest in architecture. He came from a wealthy background, and had great family support. Coco must have thought that he was not in touch with women, not real women, not in the way that she was; she understood them naturally and criticised them just as naturally. She thought these new designers would never share the same connection with women that she had. They were too lost in their own worlds, too detached from reality, with their educations and endless financial possibilities.

In 1925, Dior decided to study political science with the idea of finding work as a diplomat. However, after his graduation, his father decided to support his passion and lend him the money he needed to open his own gallery. He was not thrilled about his son's decision to start a more creative career but decided to support him no matter what, although he made it clear that Christian was not to use the family name for his new venture. Thanks to his new gallery, Dior soon started to connect with the most interesting artists of the time, handling the work of Picasso, Georges Braques, Jean Cocteau and Max Jacob. He was forced to close the gallery in 1931 after his family experienced financial and emotional troubles as a consequence of his father's business shutting down and his older brother and mother dying. In spite of this, he had, already succeeded in making a name for himself, and he had done so with some of the most respected artists of the time. With the closure of his gallery, Dior went through a hard time and, he began to do whatever was in his power to survive by using what he did best; sketching was one of his talents and he decided to sell fashion sketches. It was a success, fashion was something he clearly knew how to bring to the paper and in 1935, he managed to get a job at the *Figaro Illustré*, it was the start of a bright career in the fashion world and years later, he also managed to land a job as a design assistant for Robert Piguet, a Paris fashion designer.

Despite Coco's ideas, Dior was not simply a spoiled child supported by his family but someone who would not shy away from work, and when the Second World War broke, he was one of the many Parisian men to serve as an officer in the French army. During the war and the French occupation by Germany in 1940, Dior made his way back to Paris and started to work with another fashion designer, Lucien Lelong, while his own sister, Catherine became involved in the French Resistance.

His health was not the best, and in 1957, months after appearing on the cover of *Time* magazine, Dior decided to take a holiday in Italy, in Montecassini where he died on 23 October after suffering from a heart attack (his third one). He was only 52, and a private plane was sent by French entrepreneur Marcel Boussac and Dior's body was brought back to Paris where his funeral was attended by over 2,500 people.

Coco and Balenciaga

Coco admired Balenciaga and one night, after a few drinks, she asked him to marry her, half joking, half serious, she was a woman who had arrived in her eighties with no true companion and she must have felt the weight of that solitude. Balenciaga was a man whose work she truly loved, whose classic designs and dream-like gowns inspired many, Coco included. Cristobal Balenciaga was born in 1895 in Guetaria, Spain, and had shown a strong passion for fashion and dressmaking from the age of 10. He did not come from a wealthy family, his father was a sea captain and his mother had started working as a seamstress to support the family.

It is reported that his father died prematurely and that his mother took even more work on to make ends meet, he was an only child and used to spend whole afternoons with her, looking at her work, copying what she did; several stories about this early time in his life describe a Balenciaga open and willing to learn more about the fashion world; he was often found admiring women's clothes in the street, including those of a local aristocrat, the Marquesa de Cast Torres; legend says that she invited him to make a copy of the same tailleur.

His childhood mirrored Coco's in a way as his father was not in the picture either, and his mother had worked as a seamstress. Romantic and a bit of a dreamer, Coco no doubt loved the fact that Balenciaga's father was a sea captain, someone she would have only read about in one of her favourite books. Balenciaga made his very first trip to Paris when he was 15; he was so taken by the Parisian mood, even the air was different then, that he decided to become a fashion designer and by the time he was 20, he had opened his very first fashion boutique and laboratory in Spain. He was for the Spanish what Coco was for the French, he quickly attracted extensive praise, sealing his reputation as Spain's leading fashion name.

When the Spanish Civil War broke out in 1937, Balenciaga moved his business to Paris where he met Coco Chanel, competition was fierce but the two built up a relationship based on mutual respect. His style was different to Coco's as he liked his collections and designs to be sumptuous, elegant and, somewhat, flowing. He had a predilection for capes and clothing with no waistlines, especially in the 1950s, he was one of the first to use plastic for rainwear in the 1960s. He had this ability to adapt his designs and works to the world, keeping his clothes up to date with the latest trends, something that Coco didn't do as well. In an interview, Karl Lagerfeld said that Mademoiselle Chanel had made two mistakes after coming back from her self-exile in Switzerland: she had declared herself against both the miniskirt and the use of denim, something which had taken the world by storm and something which both the press and customers all over the world did not forgive.

Balenciaga and Coco shared a similar personality and neither of them was very keen on the press, although Coco was a little softer when it came to talking to journalists, as she appreciated their influence and she would release interviews from time to time; and she managed to establish a respectful relationship with both the French and the international press. Balenciaga on the other hand didn't want to waste his time talking about his collections; much like Coco, his life was all about his work as a designer, he didn't want to do anything else and didn't see any point in even trying. He was actually famous for starting working on new collections while his fashion shows were still being held in the next room, he would just close himself in his office and start working while the press was outside waiting for him to come out and give them something to talk about. At the same time, Coco was one of the most hardworking businesswomen of her time, she would work night and day, always planning her next move, always anticipating where her business would go and how to better be at service of women and fashion. The difference was that Balenciaga seemed cold, almost indifferent to the press and anything they could say about him, while Coco needed validation. After Coco's big comeback after the Second World War, when her collections were admired by the American press, she was rumoured to complain about the French press and lament the fact that she was not as appreciated in France anymore; she was hurt, she wanted to be loved and to find the media's approval.

Balenciaga, who was a perfectionist like Coco, also believed in adding a wow factor to all his creations, luxury superseded practicality in his work. However, despite his several relationships, both Balenciaga and Coco had given their heart to fashion, there was no place, no room and definitely, no time for anyone or anything else. Despite his innovative collections, Balenciaga was behind one of the most well-crafted tailoring looks, and that made him a perfect match to Coco who had always been the queen of the tailoring look giving women a shape which embraced their silhouettes. Coco and Balenciaga had a strong friendship which lasted almost until the end; 'One day we were friends, the next we were not,' Balenciaga would say later. Many stories were told, and they probably weren't all accurate. Many tried to explain the reason behind the end of their friendship; according to several biographers including Madsen, during an interview with the press, Coco had told a journalist that she had seen Balenciaga looking tired, more tired than usual, after completing his last collection; maybe it was just something said carelessly, without meaning to discredit her good friend. Coco apologised but Balenciaga did not forgive, ending their friendship. Balenciaga was a private, introverted man who cherished privacy and had probably seen in Coco's gossiping to the press about his mood and health a breach of trust, something he could not forgive. It is difficult to establish whether Coco had wanted to discredit the only designer she felt as a true competitor, but it is probable she did not mean any harm.

Just like Coco, Balenciaga was one of the last designers to work directly on the body, he would spend hours making sure his designs fitted models perfectly and because of his perfectionism, he was also rumoured to suffer from insomnia and anxiety. He spent his whole life looking to achieve that perfect tailored look, something that he first experienced during the early years of his career, when he would take trips to Paris to buy clothes from some of the most iconic fashion houses including Vionnet, Lelong, Schiaparelli and of course, Chanel. He had received a Catholic education, like Coco, and gave to his work, the same rigour he had been taught, even French designer André Courrèges, once compared working with Balenciaga to the same work novices undergo for holy orders. Coco was particularly in awe of Balenciaga, and in all her conversations and interviews released, she would never include him with Dior and the other designers she did not admire; she strongly believed that those designers with their big and attraction-grabbing designs were not doing women any favour and surely, not exalting their beauties and features but purely covering them under complicated, unwearable shapes.

Coco believed that Balenciaga was one of the best designers when it came to cut and sew and that his technical skills were like no one else's. Unlike Coco, he was a fan of the female form and was not interested in creating designs for women who were too thin. His saleswomen would even reassure his customers if they were found to have put on a little weight between fittings. He did not like attention and was too shy to talk to the customers or the press, which, he decided to ban from one of his shows in 1947. He and Coco shared a lot; a similar background, the same principles, a love for a tailored look and an aversion to any PR stunt and to anything that would take the attention away from the designs, from their work; they shared an almost maniacal attachment, love and passion to work, the concept that clothes did not have to cover women but suit them perfectly, like something designed, created and fitted just for them. They also shared the absence of any consistent, constant relationship. Their kinship was based on the fact that they were two of the very best designers of their day and they had each wedded themselves to their fashion house. This was the only union that truly mattered to them.

Coco and Saint Laurent

The relationship between Coco and Yves Saint Laurent was highly contradictory. On one side, Coco knew that at some point she would have to give up her fashion spot as an icon and a myth, potentially to someone younger, yet she was not ready to do that. She was not ready to give up on the house of Chanel, on herself, she was the incredible fashion designer who had come back and made a name for herself once again and most certainly, she was not ready to leave her spot to Saint Laurent. Yves was young and inexperienced and yet he brought with him the power of youth, something that Coco had lost, and several times, she would accuse him of copying her style, her designs, and her very essence. However, it was not as much as a copy but more proof of Saint Laurent's admiration; after all, designers inspire each other and there was a fifty years gap in age between them, Saint Laurent admired Coco. And although she was never a fan of Saint Laurent, before her death, she admitted that she did consider him her heir, if she had to choose one.

Yves Saint Laurent was born in 1936 in Oran, Algeria. One of his very first experiences was with designer Christian Dior, thanks to this time, he managed to acquire a great reputation as a designer. He became so highly sought after in the eyes of the French press and customers that in 1966, he also created his own fashion label. In many ways, Yves and Coco had much in common, it is often said that Coco had given women freedom, freedom to be who they wanted to be, and the freedom to express themselves, Yves had given them the power to take that freedom and do whatever they wanted to do with it.

Yves Saint Laurent grew up in a villa by the Mediterranean with his parents and two younger sisters, his father was a lawyer who also owned a chain of cinemas and the family was wealthy. However, Saint Laurent was bullied as a child as most people suspected he was gay, and as a result, he grew up to be lonely and quite nervous. He showed a love for fashion from the very beginning and when he was a child, he used to design dresses for his mother and sisters. His mother who had seen a talent in him from the very beginning, decided to take him to Paris and had him enrol at La Chambre Syndicale de la Couture in Paris and later he was introduced to Dior by Michael de Brunhoff, the editor of *French Vogue*.

Saint Laurent started to work for Dior straightaway and he would always speak warmly of the years he had spent training with him; that was probably why Coco, who could hardly stomach Dior and his designs, was not exactly thrilled about Saint Laurent. When talking about Dior, he often said that he absolutely fascinated and intimidated him and that he could hardly say a word in his presence. It was under Dior that Yves Saint Laurent got the recognition he yearned for and he decided to launch his own label.

But in 1960, he was called back to Algeria to fight for its independence, something he managed to avoid because of health issues. By the time he got back to Paris, his job was gone and that pushed him to sue and win against his former boss, Dior, for breach of contract. With the money, he managed to launch his own fashion house with his partner in both work and life, Pierre Berge, and he became an icon of style, launching several new additions to a woman's closet, from his sheer blouse to the jumpsuit. Saint Laurent was a genius and an artist and would go through different dark phases in his life, battling several addictions including alcohol and cocaine. In the 1990s, after a particularly delicate moment in his career, he succeeded in making an important comeback with his designs becoming once again objects of style and desire for many. He eventually sold the company and returned to Marrakech.

He passed away in Paris in 2008 after an illness.

Coco and Poiret

Coco Chanel and Paul Poiret had one of those love-hate relationships. Much like Coco, Poiret was one of the most appreciated fashion designers of his time, he was partial to anything that was new and innovative and he was also responsible for freeing women from the corset; he also created the catwalk to showcase new designs to journalists and potential customers. He was also the first designer to launch his own fragrance, much to Coco's annoyance. Poiret was one of the first designers to realise that fashion houses were not enough anymore and that he had to expand his business further; that is why he decided to open different sections of his business including interiors and accessories offshoots. Like Coco, he was very close to artists and personalities of the time and much like Mademoiselle Chanel, he was inspired by them and inspired by their art.

Many see Poiret as the father of Art Deco. He founded his fashion house in 1904 after working for Charles Frederick Worth and he was supported by his wife and then muse, Denise, for all his life; he was the one to bring bright designs, inspired by Arabian Nights and by the costumes of the infamous Ballets Russes company, something which boasted Coco's involvement as well. He became a friend and supporter of many different artists who would later be part of the Art Deco movement; this original and quirky group featured the likes of Constantin Brancusi, Pablo Picasso, Robert Delaunay, Paul Iribe, Henri Matisse and Amedeo Modigliani. His collaboration with Iribe had the benefit of positioning him on the Art Deco map of French personalities thanks to Iribe's illustrations of Poiret's designs. Later, he also decided to work with painter Raoul Dufy to create his new in-house stationery, he was also a patron and a lover of the arts and he owned a commercial gallery, Barbazanges, where Picasso first introduced Le Demoiselles D'Avignon to the world in 1911.

Poiret was a Parisian through and through and he is remembered for his love of neoclassical and orientalist styles, as well as for the introduction of the hobble skirt, a tight, fitted skirt.

He would often say: 'I freed the bust,' referring to the time when he had liberated women from the corset, 'and I shackled the legs.'

His was a one of a kind, extravagant, excessive look and he was especially famous for his theatrical designs. His popularity started to decline after the First World War, as more and more people had become addicted to the Chanel look and started to leave excess behind in exchange for her minimalism. After Coco had created the little black dress, it is reported that Poiret used to make fun of her when bumping into her in the street, asking her why she was wearing such a sad, mournful colour all the time and why she had encouraged women all over Paris to opt for the same shade. She used to answer, 'because I am your funeral'. Compared to Coco, Poiret was exotic, extravagant and not afraid to use colours or bold shapes, while Coco was always measured, contained and a little too Chanel. There was no comparison, their styles were different, yet they were in competition and it became clear that Poiret was the past while Coco became the future. After having to close his fashion house, he said that Chanel had created the luxury version of the poor style, as luxury as it could get, it still remained poor.

Chapter 10

Coco, the End

After the Second World War, Chanel went through a different phase in her life, something she had experienced before, as she started to feel detached from the world she had known since she was a young girl with an eye for a good fabric cut and endless style. She felt different and as usual, when she felt like that, it meant that change was coming.

In Paris, in her beloved Paris, she was the Nazi, she was the one who had, apparently, befriended German soldiers, so that she could keep her lifestyle and status, someone who could not be trusted, not anymore. She was the anti-Semite, the one who had sued the Jewish brothers over an apparently trivial matter of money but who clearly or in the eye of the public had only done so for her anti-Semitic ideals.

In this divisive, suffocating mood, Coco decided to leave Paris for a while and moved to Switzerland to spend some time there; to recharge and take a pause from the horrors of the world and all the public scrutiny she had been subjected to; she thought she could do with a break, and wanted to go somewhere where she could ideally regenerate and come back, maybe, even stronger than before.

Dincklage, her lover, younger and beloved, followed her there. They had been separated after the war, but she had found that he was still alive in Hamburg. Coco, being Coco, did whatever it took, whatever she could in her power, with her connections, to get him safe and sound to Switzerland where she was, and where together, they could, maybe, start again. Dincklage had been taken to a prisoner of war camp and, at the time, he was not doing well, he was sick, and so she took him with her and nursed him back to health. The strange Franco-German couple had the chance to spend rather more peaceful years in Lausanne where

Coco made sure to reunite the rest of her family as well; including her nephew André and his wife and two daughters, Gabrielle and Helene. André and his family, alongside Adrienne, were the only family she had left or, even better, the only family Coco acknowledged and recognised as such. She had lost touch with her brothers and despite having several great nephews and great-nieces from Alphonse's son, she blatantly and consciously decided to ignore them all. As far as she told the media, the public and the people who were the closest to her, she had very little family left.

It is exactly during this time spent in Switzerland that Coco embraced a more peaceful lifestyle and started to get even closer with Paul Morand and his wife, Helene; but close doesn't even explain her relationship with Morand, as she made him one of her few intimate friends, and a keeper of her memories. When she decided to tell Morand her story, she knew that one day that same story would come out, and in many ways, she knew that she had to give a little push, a little direction to the narrative she had created for her entire life; so that she could keep her authority, her voice on her final biography. She started from her very first memories, her family, the aunts, she told Morand about them and skillfully went through some of the most important passages in her life and the most important men, including Capel and Westminster. She wasn't shy about mentioning some of her most interesting connections as well name-dropping the likes of Picasso or Stravinsky, creating what she must have thought would have made a good story to read.

Morand wrote and then wrote some more, but Coco's memoirs by Morand were put aside, maybe under direct direction from Coco herself; Morand's notes were briefly forgotten to only be re-discovered after the death of la Mademoiselle.

Coco was enjoying life in Switzerland, it was calmer, quiet and less hectic than the one she had left behind in Paris; she was not completely unhappy yet she was a businesswoman, someone who had to always busy herself with something new, a new collection, a new project or a new fragrance perhaps. Eventually, even the legal action with the Wertheimer brothers over the profits made by Chanel N°5 came to an end and

Coco celebrated the settlement with a bottle of champagne; finally, she had been given what she wanted. Now, what was she supposed to do with all that money? She was rich beyond anything she could have ever imagined yet she was not completely fulfilled; she knew that something was missing.

Coco had, finally obtained everything she wanted: the man, a good-looking man, a younger man who clearly adored her and was ready to follow her everywhere she went; she still had her prestige, her reputation, despite everything; despite whatever had happened, she would always be Chanel. She could have stopped there, retired in Switzerland and let her fashion house die with her.

She decided not to.

She was not made for taking long holidays, she felt exiled from Paris, from the rest of the world, especially the fashion world, which was moving at such a speed that she felt she could hardly keep up with it. She felt that men, new designers, male designers were taking the reins of the fashion world; men who clearly never wore what they designed and could not have been, in her mind, in touch with women and their needs. Men who had clearly never worked a single day as a seamstress and knew nothing about fabric. Yes, men had invaded the world of fashion bringing their impractical dresses and Coco was not happy about it; she was particularly furious with designers like Christian Dior who were contaminating fashion with their big, highly impractical designs. Self-banned, self-exiled in Switzerland, she felt that she was wasting her time; she hated the fact that she could not play her part, influence fashion, Parisian fashion, the way she had always done. Yes, she had been accused of being a spy and making a German soldier her lover, but did she really deserve not to be involved in the fashion world anymore?

At the same time, women in Paris were going through a different phase, times had changed and they were finally embracing modernity and what it brought; they had stopped searching for a simple, tailored look, they had stopped looking for the simplicity of the Chanel cut and were now after something more extravagant, something that would have made them forget all about the traumas of the Second World War, something that would have made them light, superficial and beautiful again; something which certainly looked a little bit more Dior than Chanel. They were not interested in whatever Coco had proposed more than a decade before; the woman who had given them the chance to be elegant yet practical was of no interest to them anymore; they were in search of a new identity, something that the new designers, male designers, were more than eager to provide.

When she and Dincklage split up in 1950, Coco started to spend more time in France, she wasn't ready to leave Switzerland just yet, she had made many friends there including Marguerite Nametalla van Zuylen who was married to Baron Egmont Van Zuylen van Nyevelt, and she also needed a plan. In 1953, Coco decided to go to the United States so that she could have a look at the new New York offices of Les Perfums Chanel; the offices were a perfect mixture of French chairs and beige carpets, she added a few touches to their interiors by having several paintings added to their wall for extra decor; she chose Henri Rousseau and Auguste Renoir.

She spent three months in New York, she must have felt re-energised, she loved working, and she loved her business. She began to reflect a little more seriously on the possibility of reopening the Chanel house. She was not ready to leave fashion and especially the elegant Parisian fashion in the hands of those men; they had no idea what they were doing, they didn't know how to run a fashion house or how to come up with a collection. She was also particularly shocked that they did not work directly on the models, something that she absolutely loved doing, but that they merely sketched, how were they supposed to see what they were creating? Coco was a designer who modelled her creations directly on the body and she couldn't understand how anyone could have done anything differently.

She could also hardly see the point of creating such extravagant clothes, something women could not wear on social occasions as they were so inconvenient.

Supported by her friend Maggy's daughter, Marie Helene de Rothschild, she decided to reopen the Chanel house and offer her services once again to the women of Paris, saving them in her head from the savage designers of her time. She was 70.

But how did she make that decision?

It happened by chance, the way it had always happened with Coco; something that must have taken her back to the time when she had made hats for Balsan's friends. One night, Marie Helene had bought a big, excessive gown for a party she was supposed to attend. Coco had given one look at the gown and had decided that it was not suited to the event. She had taken matter in her own hands and had crafted her a new dress out of a big curtain in crimson taffeta. Everyone at the party had been raving about the dress and begging Marie Helene to reveal the name of her designer.

In an obituary compiled by *The New Yorker*, Marie Helene de Rothschild was described as one of Europe's most imaginative hostesses, she was a socialite and she also shared her mother's fierce personality and eclectic taste in fashion. Her husband, Baron Guy de Rothschild, was the dean of the French brand of the famous banking family, something that Coco must have taken in high regard. Marie Helene was highly regarded as a socialite in the Parisian circle and could often be spotted at dinners, balls and galas she would carefully organise; most of her *soirees* had as their beautiful location the Chateau Ferriers, which was a former Rothschild mansion. She was, in many ways, a younger, prettier Misia Sert and Coco could not help but being her friend and taking her under her wing; or maybe it was Marie Helene who took the French designer under her wing, pushing her to come back and be, once again, the talented, most acclaimed fashion designer she had always been.

Marie Helene was an eclectic character, a real personality of her time, someone who clearly did a lot for Coco and who loved to surround herself with the best social circle. She was rumoured once to have sent out dinner invitations that had to be read with a mirror. She loved nothing more than shocking people with her dresses and parties and once, she hosted a party for more than sixteen hundred people, completely covering Ferrieres with white muslin. Marie Helene had a strong personality, and could not be tamed, and Coco must have recognised those traits in her. They had several things in common and Coco loved surrounding herself with strong women. She also had friends of different ages, and it is no surprise that she was a very good friend of Marie Helene and both her parents as well.

With Ferrieres having been donated to the government, Marie Helene kept her social life in the French capital and that is when she and Coco became even closer; with Marie Helene becoming a more prominent figure in the Chanel universe. A socialite through and through, Marie Helene also loved to entertain influential figures from both the aristocracy and show business, including Elizabeth Taylor, Princess Grace, the Duchess of Windsor, Yves Saint Laurent, Oscar de la Renta and even Andy Warhol. She loved to mix different people at her parties, sparking interesting conversations. She was often described by her friends as being extraordinarily intelligent, curious and open to new ideas and experiences. Later in her life, she even worked as an interior decorator, another thing she had in common with Coco. Marie Helene was also a natural when it came to fashion and became one of the most prominent supporters of the French couture and in 1973, she became president of the committee that was behind the Divertissement a Versailles; a major event where American designers were given the chance to showcase their works in the European market.

Thanks to her connections, charisma and personality, Marie Helene supported Coco and her comeback; she gave her the little push she needed in order to grab once again the reins of her fashion house. Coco welcomed the support, but she also had a plan in mind already.

The truth was no matter how long she had stayed away from the fashion scene, she was still Coco and yes, her designs were still as timeless as herself or so she thought.

She got herself back to the Ritz and sold her beautiful villa at Roquebrune, she didn't need it anymore, she needed to get back to being herself, to being Coco Chanel, and the only way she knew how to do that was through her first love: fashion.

She returned to Paris. She was back.

Of course, she had acknowledged the competition, it had become fierce and a little part of her felt that she had been away from the fashion scene for too long, exiled, ostracised, and ever diminishing in influence.

She felt like she was missing something, and so she worked even harder on her comeback. Ideally, she wanted to find an American buyer, someone who could have taken the Chanel experience to the American ladies. She worked hard and kept her collection pretty secretive, she also managed to secure once again the help of the Wertheimers. They wanted to see Chanel N°5 performing better in the market; and they had hoped that by re-launching the Chanel fashion house, a butterfly effect would have touched Chanel N°5, helping sales to pick up.

Despite the support, the money and all the work, her first fashion show did not find the success she had hoped for. The media was bitter and unforgiving; she was certainly different than what they had been used to; Coco was no Dior and she was not offering them the allure of his extravagances. Her collection was simple, too simple, nothing that excited or outraged the media or the public. She had planned everything extremely carefully from the selection of the models to the interiors, the decor of the room itself, everything had been perfect, immaculate in perfect Chanel style but it had not been enough for the press, it had not been the biggest comeback of the season, as many had predicted. According to many, her collection was a reheated soup, and certainly, not the sensationalism they had grown accustomed to. Perhaps they would have criticised her no matter what she did, maybe the French public was still bitter about her past sympathies, her lovers and rumoured Nazi friends; maybe they resented her arrogance or the fact that she had been tainted by anti-Semitism her whole life.

Some of the most acclaimed newspapers of the time said that it had been like stepping back to the roaring twenties and that was certainly not meant as a compliment. Many accused her of being too old-fashioned, of belonging to the past, several concluded that she had nothing else to say, nothing more to add to the fashion world, she was subtly or not so subtly accused of having recreated a collection which had nothing special to offer and was not of any use to the fashion world in Paris or anywhere else. Several London-based newspapers were also very harsh, with the *Daily Express* describing her fashion show an 'utter fiasco'.

To the outside world, Coco certainly seemed detached from the latest trends, clearly expressing her disdain at the direction fashion was then heading. According to Madsen, Simon Baron, a London critic, managed to speak to her about the show's reception. She professed herself to be absolutely shocked, and she made sure to express her vision once again by speaking the truth, her truth. She made dresses, clothes, for women, she believed women deserved something wearable, comfortable but overall chic that would make them stand out. She said that her main goal was not to please the couture house or the media, that was not what her job was, she was there for women; after all, she had been the one liberating them from tight corsets (or she claimed); she had been the one, to give them a different way of seeing themselves. Overall, she could not accept the media and her critics' opinions, and fully rejected their point of view. She was after all Coco Chanel and the Chanel House would not have changed its vision because someone told them to. She vowed not to give up, she was going to keep going and thanks to Pierre Wertheimer who kept backing her financially, that was exactly what she did.

Later on, after a more successful fashion season, *Life* magazine published an article singing the praises of Mademoiselle Chanel and how she could never get it wrong, the French and the European press followed shortly after; and from that moment on, she was back, and no one could question her role in the fashion world anymore. From then on, she simply kept doing what she did best – never sketching but instead, working directly on the body. She went to dress some of the most important actresses and women of her time, icons of beauty and style, including Grace Kelly, Sophia Loren and Catherine Deneuve. The stars, those who seriously counted in Hollywood, almost exclusively wore Chanel. She was Coco Chanel and her name became a synonym of everything that was chic, tailored and elegant; women started to have a choice when it came to fashion, it was all about them, and who they wanted to be. If they wanted to be extravagant and eclectic, they went to Dior. But for those who favoured effortless chic, then Chanel was their designer.

Coco was once again in the public eye, she was making the news, customers kept coming, not everyone but it did not matter; women bought a Chanel when they had a specific look in mind, they did not go to Chanel expecting the irreverence of Dior, they went to Chanel when they wanted to be a Chanel woman. Fashion had changed, more styles were available, and women finally could be whoever they wanted to be. Coco knew this, she knew that she could count on women, she knew that, as much as she didn't like women, women liked her, her designs and anything she stood for.

She was back, her creative, irreverent, caustic, sarcastic self was back and she was not going away, she became someone constantly interviewed by the press, her thoughts, her opinions on fashion, on life, on women and men became highly regarded in the eye of the media. People listened to what she had to say, her words became mottos, gentle reminders of what women should always try to aspire to. She often found herself talking about the reasons she hadn't married, and she would admit that she had fallen in love with two different men who had to tried to own her, to take her away from what she knew, loved and was good at; and, despite her love, despite how desperately she had been in love with them both, she had seen herself forced to say goodbye. The two men she kept referring to her entire life were Capel and Westminster. They had tried to own her, but she wasn't a woman to be mastered. She was her job and her designs. She was the House of Chanel.

She became more and more creative, France was not enough, Paris was too small, she went on to conquer the US with the Americans raving about her collections and her incredible taste. She expanded her business further, and decided to launch a second perfume, it was meant to be for men, but it wasn't a typical musty, male scent. She wanted to call it Coco but the Wertheimers were not happy about that, as they believed the name wasn't catchy enough. She ended up calling it Five, her favourite number and her day of birth.

Despite the turmoil of an incredibly busy life for a woman who was way over 80, she started to suffer from depression and would often complain about being lonely.

To Gabrielle Palasse, one of the few relatives she had kept in touch with, she would complain about her lonely life, about not having a family of her own.

She spent her days working herself silly and later in her life, she became a little more introspective; that same introspection that she had only experienced as a child, she took to spending more and more time in cemeteries as she had done when she was younger. She felt that the tombstones gave her the peace she yearned for and made her feel a little less lonely. She got very close to Claude Baillen, her psychologist friend, who accompanied her during those lonely walks and was always at her side, whenever Coco needed her. Later, Baillen also went on to publish a memoir about Coco. Coco started to tell her the story of her life, half-erasing family members and only acknowledging Julia as her sister.

She felt the weight of age and later death looming over her and with almost no family around, she decided to surround herself with people she could trust; she hired new servants, including Francois Mironnet, who together with her maid Celine became everything to her, confidante, helper and even business consultant.

According to biographer Vaughan, Coco's fortune was held in trust by Coga, the foundation she had created before her death, and administered by Gabrielle Palasse Labrunie, her niece.

In his biography, Vaughan also spoke about the role Francois Mironnet played after Mademoiselle Chanel's death. Mironnet together with Céline whom she called Jeanne like her mother, and her secretary Lilou Grumbach, who worked as a butler for Coco until the very end were all very close to their mistress. Mironnet often sat with her to eat together or played cards with Lilou while Mademoiselle slept in the next room.

After Coco's death, Mironnet produced a letter as a proof to claim part of Coco's fortune which included a large sum of money as well as her house in Switzerland. According to Vaughan, many intellectuals of the time such as Jean Cau, former secretary of Jean-Paul Sartre, took Mironnet's side in the dispute.

Despite the letter being exhibited in court, the entire matter was settled privately between Coco's niece Gabrielle and Mironnet.

Coco began suffering from sleepwalking, and apparently, she begged her beloved, most faithful models to chain her to the bed, making sure she wouldn't walk, or embarrass herself in the middle of the night. All her life, she had been taking morphine which she kept injecting herself until the very last days, something which was a little reminder of her most hedonic years. She would only spend time with Claude Baillen, preferring her own company to anyone else, nevertheless, the two became inseparable.

Her 1971 Spring fashion show was yet another success, especially with American ladies who were raving about Chanel and her designs; but success was not enough, it was never going to be enough, and Coco was tired, Mademoiselle was lonely.

She could feel the years that had gone by, she could feel the change, she could also equally feel the pace shifting, yet she still felt like herself, she was still Coco, or was she?

She became quiet, introverted, careful around people, not letting strangers in, not even some members of her own family, people she did not want around. Alphonse's daughters came to visit once and she had her maid turn them away, they tried and tried to convince the maid that they were not seeking money or anything, they just wanted to meet their aunt, maybe for the first time since they had been born.

It had become increasingly difficult to create collections that would stand out in a world that was becoming more and more competitive; in a world which clamoured to shock; a world that started to move a little forward and to focus on other designers, other styles, including the ever-present, Elsa Schiaparelli, Coco's frenemy and most important competitor.

It became way too much, the solitude, the old age. Betrayed by a sick body, trapped in her own fabrications, the romantic heroine had started to fade.

It became way too much, the solitude, the old age. Betrayed by a sick body, trapped in her own fabrications, the romantic heroine had started to fade. She died the way she had lived, like a diva or a goddess, in her suite at the Ritz, with Celine, by her side. She had worked all that week, but something hadn't been right for quite some time. Her figure had become even more slender, she hardly ate anything and complained about food smells all the time; her smell, once one of her most precious assets, had turned into an enemy. All of a sudden, she cried that she could not breathe, she urged Celine to open a window, a doctor was called but it was a Sunday and he did not come soon enough or maybe it would not have made a single difference.

In many ways, Mademoiselle Chanel died like the romantic heroine she had been her entire life with the most romantic words on her lips, as reported by Celine:

'You see, this is how you die.'

She could not have said something more perfect if she had tried.

Chapter 11

Coco, the Icon, the Rebel, the Myth

A popular TV advert comes to mind. Keira Knightly with a garçon haircut, a beige jumpsuit runs on a motorcycle in Paris. *This is a Man's World* chants her journey as she attends a photoshoot in rue Cambon, another busy day in her manic yet alluring life.

She is Coco, a Coco of our time, she is what Coco would have been if she had been born later, a true businesswoman of our time, who knew what she wanted and wasn't afraid to work hard and then even harder in order to get it.

We have been told that she was a rebel. She was the one refusing Aubazine and its conventions, she was the designer behind the little black dress and Chanel N°5, she was the lover, the friend, the patron, the woman many desired but could not really have, she was a rebel of her time and still one of ours.

She embraced the Parisian society of the time, yet she tried to create something new, developing collections that were appreciated by ordinary people, whilst remaining practical yet beautiful. Everyone wanted to know about her, they wanted to find out about her, to know who she was and where she was from and how she had managed to not only create a business but also to give women an alternative, different choice when it came to fashion.

She had also become an icon, an icon who would create other icons, supporting them personally and financially; her acquaintances, her friends who benefitted from her taste, finance and support. In terms of creativity, she had been lucky enough to live during one of the most intense moments in history, and those she encountered became icons of their own, shaping and nurturing popular trends.

But how did this wonderfully talented woman become an icon? It wasn't a straightforward path and it took years for Coco and the House of Chanel to establish themselves as a bold and unforgettable fashion force. At first, Coco became a pivotal personality in Paris, someone others would look at, someone people would aspire to be, someone whose taste would inspire some of the most beautiful and desired women of the world. She established a strong reaction in those she met; people were equally fond and scared of her.

She was the woman behind some of the most iconic moments in fashion, she created the garçon look, the little black dress, and Chanel N°5. Everything in her appearance from the short hair to the Breton t-shirt and the infamous black dress became iconic, something so effortless and chic that it soon became a new classic uniform for women; with her little black dress and white pearls, as any other colour would have been, almost, tasteless, becoming a statement of elegance and chic of their own.

Like most icons, she was rarely portrayed positively by the press. Instead she was deeply demonised. Her apparent involvement with the Nazi regime during the occupation of Paris, her fight with the Wertheimer brothers and her alleged anti-Semitism did not help. She was also, always, bitterly, criticised for being partial to slender figures; once while questioned about the fact that she did not have children, she said that she had not wanted children for fear of putting on too much weight and being considered too heavy in the arms of a man. Yet, what essentially made her an icon were her creations, tangible proof of her innate sense of fashion and aesthetics; she created iconic fashion moments which stood the test of time and still today, are considered some of her best creations.

Coco and the LBD

Coco was the stylish force behind the very first little black dress. At the time, black was something for people who were going through mourning, and it was most certainly not regarded as being elegant let alone, chic.

Coco made little black dresses an essential statement garment in any women's wardrobe. Elegant, and chic, Coco was famous for saying: 'Simplicity is the keynote of all elegance' and also 'Fashion fades, only style remains the same,' and her style, her simple style most definitely remained.

The little black dress, often called, LBD, made its first apparition as an illustration in *American Vogue* and was instantly called 'the ford' dress by its editors after the classic black car, which was very popular at the time.

The dress was different from anything else women had worn before, it was fitted, perfectly embraced the silhouette and being black, it suited everyone.

Coco wears trousers

Coco was also one of the first women to ever wear trousers. At the time, only men wore trousers but Coco who was often accused of behaving like a man, mostly by Capel, refused to work in skirts, turning her back once again on patriarchal conventions. She loved wearing trousers and overalls especially when she was working, as these were more practical and, also, more business-like for when she had meetings; it was a more business-like uniform she embraced, something people would have seen and instantly associated with someone who deserved to be taken seriously, usually men. Later on, trousers became a necessity for women when doing more practical activities, being outdoors or just doing sports.

Coco and jersey

The idea for the jersey fabric came to her one hot summer in Biarritz when she was young and in love with Boy Capel, it was a new, fascinating and highly practical concept destined to change and revamp the world of fashion.

Jersey was, often, a fabric which was used for men's underwear, no one would have ever thought of Jersey as a new fabric to use for women's fashion, no one would have dared. Yet Coco was determined to take advantage of the situation, she strived for innovation and was ready to give women what they needed, rather than what they wanted, keeping costs down. That is exactly how she dissed some of the most well-known and highly sought fabrics, which included satins and skins, in favour of the jersey.

She always said she wanted to make life easier for women and so she did.

Coco and The Chanel

A Chanel bag, the 2.55 handbag, to be precise, was another iconic fashion moment for the Chanel House. Coco was looking for a bag that would free the arms, and once again, she was inspired by the men's world, after all, everything was much easier and more practical for them. She was determined to give women the same level of practicality and comfort; she first had a look at soldiers' bags and found herself captivated by the use of the straps. She quickly decided to add tiny straps to her first Chanel bag and, later on, she updated her own design and created the 2.55.

N°5

It would be impossible to talk about Coco's most iconic moments without mentioning Chanel N°5, a perfume that was born out of her love for fragrances with a pinch of an adoration she had for everything that was mystical and slightly supernatural.

It was such an iconic moment for Coco, and the beginning of a new era, the era of the Chanel women. At the time, Coco was going through an extremely passionate phase in her life, as she was dating Grand Duke Dmitri Pavlovich. It was thanks to her lover that she made the acquaintance of a Russian perfumer, Ernest Beaux. She had always wanted to create a perfume and when she decided to work with Beaux, she was presented with different results after the first testing phase. She naturally went for the fragrance labelled number five: 'I always launch my collection on the 5th day of the 5th months, so the number 5 seems to bring me luck – therefore, I will name it No. 5,' she said later. Chanel N°5 was the first perfume made using synthetic ingredients rather than essential oils which were the first choice traditionally. The fragrance was launched in May (5th month of the year).

In many ways, the creation of her Chanel N°5 was a rebellious moment.

Coco naturally always smelled divine and by now, we know that she used to add a few drops of Chanel N°5 to her fireplace to scent the room of her Ritz suite; to her, women must always smell wonderful. 'A woman who doesn't wear perfume has no future,' she used to say.

A girl from the South of France, a girl born in Samur, Coco had grown accustomed to beautiful smells and her main purpose was to give women a chance to always be desirable not only for men but also and mostly for themselves. She was, after all, a businesswoman, and she was always looking into different ways to improve and expand her business. She created a signature fragrance which was the anthem of the woman that she was at the time and had become; a rebellious woman, someone who would not take no for an answer, and who would do whatever in her power to succeed. Chanel N°5 stood for anything innovative, rebellious, and it was all about a woman becoming herself and conquering the business world by taking advantage of her extraordinary talent for fashion and beauty; as well as possessing a particular talent to anticipate the trends of the moment. The creation of Chanel N°5 happened just like that, randomly, by chance.

She and Ernest worked tirelessly on creating the chemical formula for a special new fragrance, taking a chance, and grabbing the opportunity to shape the women's fragrance, something that was becoming more and more important in France at the time. They sensed and perfectly understood women and the confusion they were experiencing at the time, the end of the First World War had had a strong impact on women, and their world; they were daughters of the Belle Époque, they had experienced first the beauties society had to offer and then the horror, the crude horror of the war. Women were now looking for something different, something beautiful, something Chanel.

Most importantly, they were looking for a new identity and Coco who had been crafting her own identity for her entire life was the perfect candidate for the job.

At the time, women from a more upper-class world wore traditional perfumes, they were not interested in anything too complicated, they preferred single essences and had no particular inclination in trying anything too innovative or 'out there'. They mostly wore essences made from single flowers; women from the lower classes usually preferred warmer fragrances, typically made from animal musk and jasmine.

Coco and her pearls

Coco also brought back to life the fashion of wearing jewellery, different kinds with their own story and not all precious or expensive. She wore jewellery in her daywear and became a strong advocate of pearls, even faux ones.

Coco and the Breton look

A big fan of the look herself, Coco was one of the many designers, ultimately, responsible for creating a mariniere look. While spending time on the French Riviera with Capel, her lover, she saw sailors wearing the look and decided to bring the Breton style to female fashion, inspiring countless women, including actress Brigitte Bardot.

Coco became an icon in so many different ways, you wore Chanel when you needed something classy, something that would have exuded elegance and chic, something fit for an actress but mostly a first lady.

It is not difficult to understand why two very different women, opposite to each other in style, and rumoured to have shared the same man were big fans of Chanel-inspired designs and beauty products.

One was Marylin Monroe, who by now we know would only sleep with two drops of Chanel N°5. The other was Jacqueline Kennedy, the first lady had made Chanel her own signature look. The pink Chanel suit was not just another piece of fashion, it became a landmark.

Designed by Coco in 1961 for her autumn/winter collection, the pink suit had been worn by Jacqueline Kennedy on the day her husband was brutally assassinated, the suit which is still stained with the president's blood has never been cleaned and is kept in a temperature and humidity controlled room. Jacqueline didn't change and insisted on wearing the double-breasted, pink suit through the swearing-in of Lyndon B. Johnson.

She'd chosen the outfit after her husband had told her that she had to look extra beautiful as they were going to meet many Republican women that day, and the pink suit was a favourite of the late president. Like anything Coco designed, it was conceived for the independent woman in mind, yet it was also extraordinarily feminine thanks to its sweet pink nuance.

In Conversations with David M. Lubin, Wake Forest University, author of Shooting Kennedy: JFK and The Culture of Images:

Jacqueline Kennedy: a tragic moment immortalises Chanel

'When Jackie Kennedy wore a Chanel suit or, some have maintained, an American-made imitation, in the Dallas motorcade, that item of clothing was already an international symbol of female rationality and self-assurance. Chanel suits were elegantly tailored, subtly refined, and even slightly mannish, because they were, after all, suits. Yet they were also considered feminine, especially when, as with the one Mrs Kennedy wore that morning in Dallas, they were pink. The stunned widow of the slain president refused to change out of her blood-stained jacket, blouse, and skirt when she accompanied his corpse home to Washington, DC, on Air Force One. As the plane unloaded that night, viewers around the world were shocked to witness such graphic evidence of the terrible crime. The Chanel suit is the most legendary garment in American history, a sacred relic hidden away in the vaults of the National Archive.'

Photography and its role in shaping brands

'In the 1920s, when new print technologies and economies of scale allowed weekly magazines to replace simple line drawings or colour lithographs with lavish, high-contrast photography, the fashion world took notice. Now it was possible in an array of popular magazines for advertisers to display beautiful but anonymous fashion models wearing desirable clothing. In their editorial pages, these same magazines featured luminaries of stage, screen, and sports dressed in what today we would call product placements. Simultaneously, Hollywood studios perfected a new genre of mass communication known as glamor photography to help market the movies in which these stars appeared. Fan magazines, fashion magazines, Hollywood glamor photography, the movies themselves, and a growing public fascination with celebrities and celebrity culture thus came together to make photography an indispensable arm of the fashion industry, a role it has not since relinquished.'

When a brand takes a jump and turns into an icon

'The jump only occurs when there's a rare and unexpected pairing between a specific brand and a world-historical event or transcendent figure (Jackie with Chanel, Audrey with Givenchy, James Dean with Lee Rider jeans). Even if death is involved – especially when death is involved – it's a match made in branding heaven.'

Coco was an icon capable of creating other icons who survived her and went beyond her passing; her charisma, taste and aesthetics stood the test of time and went to expand and create other icons inspired directly and indirectly by la Mademoiselle; including the man, the genius who replaced her after her death: Karl Lagerfeld.

Karl Lagerfeld, the icon, the myth, was labelled as being the master of reinvention, he had changed, transformed himself constantly, he was the creative director of Chanel, Fendi and his very own label, he was the man who had defined and redefined Chanel, its fashion and icon, after the label had been almost forgotten following Coco's death.

By the time he joined Chanel, the brand had been forgotten by the media and the public, slowly evolving into something exclusively for older women. It had lost its allure, charisma and yes, even its exclusivity. Lagerfeld was the one who successfully managed to bring the Chanel name back, re-introducing it to the modern world with a new spin; he often said he did exactly what Coco would have done herself; he understood the brand, its essence, icon and myth; he knew where it came from, yet he was not afraid to experiment, playing with the innovation that had always been at the heart of anything Coco did.

Born in 1933, Karl Otto Lagerfeld born Lagerfeldt (he changed his surname after publishing a diet book) was the son of a German businessman and a Swedish mother; he had come from a small yet close family and had two siblings, Martha Christiane, a sister born in 1931 and a half-sister, Thea, from his father's first marriage. After emigrating to Paris with his family when he was 14, he started to study drawing and history; he later became fashion designer Pierre Balmain's assistant, one of Coco's many competitors in Paris. Later, he also worked with designer Jean Patou, focusing on his haute couture collections. Karl was an icon in his own right, he was a man of many talents and interests, and much like Coco, he had a passion for theatre productions and had supported several projects as a costume designer; these included *Les Troyens* by Hector Berlioz at Milan's La Scala Theatre, *Komödie der Verführung* by Arthur Schnitzler at the Burgtheater in Vienna and *Der Schwierige* by Hugo von Hofmannsthal at the Salzburg Festival. His relationship with the theatre would inspire him and added a certain drama to his Chanel catwalk shows despite maintaining Coco's essence present and alive.

Lagerfeld could speak several languages and he was a keen reader and the owner of 7L, a bookshop in Paris; he shared his passion for books and literature with Coco whose love for books was, of course, explored in Culture Chanel. Lagerfeld worked for many designers including Krizia, Charles Jourdan and Valentino, Fendi and Chloe; and he joined the house of Chanel in 1983, ten years after Coco's death. According to *Vogue*, he was an innovator and capable of anticipating trends and moods of the moment. Much like Coco, he never felt the need to hide his partiality for slender figures and he was often criticised by the media for doing so; he, himself, had lost weight and published a diet book, he often said that fashion had given him the right motivation to do so.

He worked with several celebrities and in 2011, he designed singer Lily Allen's evening dress for her wedding to Sam Cooper. He was not interested in technology, and he once admitted that he did not like using devices and he often complained about technology interrupting his work, his creative process. He was an eclectic artist and in 2011, he worked on the collection of a glassware line for a Swedish company called Orrefors, it was a minimal collection, something which he said he had loved doing, as he adored experimenting with different forms of art. In June 2011, he received the Gordon Parks Foundation Award for his work as a designer, photographer and filmmaker. He admitted his work was never done and that he loved Gordon's photos and that they inspired him as a young student in Munchen.

Both Lagerfeld and Coco were known for their sharp quotes, here is a selection of some of their most famous, it is interesting to notice how similar their thoughts, tone and strengths were.

Lagerfeld on taking over Chanel:

'When I took over Chanel, everybody said to me, "Don't touch it. It's dead. There's nothing you can do." And I said to myself, "I love that people think that. Now let's see."'

Lagerfeld on healthy competition:

'Is there something healthier than competition? If not, you fall asleep and think success, and what you did, is granted. Nothing is granted in fashion, and this is what I love about fashion.'

Lagerfeld on social media:

'Those social networks, there's something sad about them…It's like a talkative mirror where people talk to themselves. And what I hate most in life is selfies.'

Lagerfeld on his customers:

'There was once a designer in Paris who said, "My dresses are only for intelligent women." She went out of business, so maybe there were only idiots. In fact, it was not clever for her to say that. I design for the people who like. There is no age group because age group is racism in a way, too.'

Lagerfeld on fashion:

'To say that there is no fashion anymore is ridiculous. The fashion of no-fashion is still fashion. And fashion is a train that waits for nobody. Get on it, or it's gone.'

Lagerfeld's on researching for his collections:

'I'm very curious. I read every magazine, I have spies all over the place, I know everything. Very few people are as informed as I am.'

Lagerfeld on his process:

'I design like I breathe. You don't ask to breathe. It just happens.'

Coco on style:

'In order to be irreplaceable, one must always be different.'

'Fashion is not simply a matter of clothes. Fashion is in the air, born on the wind. One intuits it. It is in the sky and on the road.'

'A girl should be two things: classy and fabulous.'

On women:

'Nature gives you the face you have at twenty. Life shapes the face you have at thirty. But at fifty you get the face you deserve.'

'"Where should one use perfume?" a young woman asked. "Wherever one wants to be kissed," I said.'

'I don't understand how a woman can leave the house without fixing herself up a little – if only out of politeness. And then, you never know, maybe that's the day she has a date with destiny. And it's best to be as pretty as possible for destiny.'

'Dress shabbily and they remember the dress; dress impeccably and they remember the woman.'

'If a man speaks badly about all women, it usually means he was burned by one woman.'

On fashion:

'Fashion passes, style remains.'

'Scheherazade is easy; a little black dress is difficult.'
'Elegance is not the prerogative of those who have just escaped from adolescence, but of those who have already taken possession of their future.'

'Fashion has become a joke. The designers have forgotten that there are women inside the dresses. Most women dress for men and want to be admired. But they must also be able to move, to get into a car without bursting their seams! Clothes must have a natural shape.'

'Nothing goes out of fashion sooner than a long dress with a very low neck.'

'Fashion is made to become unfashionable.'

Coco on beauty:

'Beauty is not prettiness: why do so many mothers teach their daughters to be affected, instead of teaching them about beauty? Its true, beauty is not learnt in a flash; but by the time you have learnt through experience, beauty has faded away! It's one of the facets of the female tragedy. There are so many others, about which novelists and those "who look into a woman's heart" are dreadfully unaware.'

Coco on books:

'Most of all, I bought books to read them. Books have been my best friends. Just as the radio is a box full of lies, so each book is a treasure. The very worst book has something to say to you, something truthful. The silliest are masterpieces of human experience. I have come across many very intelligent and highly cultivated people; they were astonished by what I knew; they would have been much more so if I had told them that I had learnt about life through novels. If I had daughters, I would give them novels for their instruction. There you find all the great unwritten laws that govern mankind. In my region of the country, people didn't speak; they were not taught through the oral tradition. From the serial novels, read in the barn by the light of a candle stolen from the maid, to the greatest classics, all novels are reality in the guise of dreams. As a child, I instinctively read catalogues like novels-novels are merely big catalogues.'

Coco and Karl, their quotes and what they said, have cemented the myth of both designers in the social media world, giving power to the idea of both Lagerfeld but most importantly Coco as two unapproachable icons of fashion and style. They might have gone but their myths remain: imperfect, bold, yet still there.

Coco's myth, in particular, was sealed with a number of representations, movies, documentaries and biographies inspired to her life and creations; Lagerfeld said he was not a fan of memoirs and was not interesting in writing one. Coco's face, the silhouette has been copied, adapted and given shape to several portraits in different media forms. Different films have been also made about her life, her love for Stravinsky explored in *Coco and Igor*, her childhood and mysterious background discussed in *Coco Avant Chanel*. Yet, most of these representations had taken inspiration from her own world, the character she had clearly played well all her life, the romantic heroine of her time.

She even died like the romantic heroine she had been, in her room at the Ritz hotel with no-one else there but her maid. The woman, the icon, the lover, the patron, who had done so much for others and her friends, died on her own.

Her myth could have died with her, it would have been easier but for a reason or another, it didn't.

Books, movies, biographies have kept the Chanel machine alive and then came Lagerfeld whose own personality, strength and love for the fashion house kept it going even longer. He made Chanel Chanel again, something which it had not been for a long time; not even after Coco's incredibly criticised comeback when she was in her seventies.

Coco became the myth and the myth became her. Hundreds came together at the Church of the Madeleine to say goodbye to the fashion icon, and many wore Chanel suits as a tribute.

Later, in 2008, a movie with Shirley MacLaine saw a televised version of the designer's movie and then, Lagerfeld came, with his beautiful fashion shows, his bold ideas, his innovation and style and in many ways, the myth of Coco started again, one last time.

It is still difficult to establish who Coco was in the end, as her name, persona and life have been so perfectly associated with her fashion house; she had become the icon and the rebel in each one of us. But who was she?

She was a woman of many passions who lived her life like someone out of a book and who later consciously made up stories, beautiful stories, to give herself a more mysterious allure. Yet, her many iconic moments, her bold personality, her fascinating life, and the interesting, eclectic people she met on her path, gave her an almost ethereal status. She was Madame Bovary, crushed by the *ennui* and always looking for something else, something better, and something that perhaps would have given her the purpose she had yearned, for something that would have made her narrative, finally, complete.

She wanted to be a heroine, but she became so much more: a myth, a fantasy, a tale to tell, and then she became the tale itself.

Bibliography

Books consulted

Berman, Constance H. The Catholic Historical Review. (2011)

Chris Greenhalgh, Coco and Igor. (Headline Publishing Group 2002)

Chaney, L. An Intimate Life. (Penguin Books 2012)

Delay, C. Chanel Solitaire. (Collins 1973)

De la Haye, A. Chanel: Couture and Industry Paperback (V&A 3 Oct 2011)

Economic and Social Conditions in France During the Eighteenth Century Henri Sée Professor at the University of Rennes Translated by Edwin H. Zeydel.

Froment, J. Culture Chanel. La Donna Che Legge. (2016)

Holmes, D. Reviewed Work: The Notorious Life of Gyp, Right-Wing Anarchist in Fin-de Siècle France by Willa Z. Silverman.

Leymarie, J. Eternal Chanel : an icon's inspiration. (Harry. N. Abrahams 2011)

Lubin, D. Shooting Kennedy: JFK and The Culture of Images (University of California Press 2003)

Madsen, A. Coco Chanel: A Biography. (Bloomsbury 1990)

Morand, P. The Allure of Chanel. (Pushkin Press 2008)

Picardie, J. Coco Chanel. (Harper Collins 2010)

Simon, L. Coco Chanel (Critical Lives) Paperback–October 1, 2011

Vaughn, H. Sleeping with The Enemy. (Vintage Publisher 2011)

Cover and Inside Pictures Credits

Cover: Description Coco Chanel and Grand Duchess Marie of Russia

Details: An impression of the royal Russian exile, Grand Duchess Marie being given a tour of Mademoiselle Chanel's salon in Paris in the early 1920s. It accompanies an excerpt from the Grand Duchess's autobiography, published in Good Housekeeping, which tells of her meeting with the designer and her idea to produce machine embroidery for her.

Source Illustration: Corinne Boyd Dillon in Good Housekeeping magazine, June 1932

Credit: Mary Evans Picture Library

Chanel mini image, Shutterstock, editorial: Editorial credit: Elena Dijour

Gabrielle Chanel Coco vector sketch portrait illustration. Shutterstock, editorial. By Natata

Inside Pictures:
Inside Pictures Credits
Coco Chanel: A New Portrait by Marion Pike (2013), Fashion Space Gallery,
London College of Fashion UAL, photographs by Daniel Caulfield-Sriklad.

Picture No	10638741
Description	Coco Chanel
Caption	Gabrielle (Coco) Chanel (1883–1971), iconic French fashion designer, pictured by her car in fashionable Biarritz.
Credit Line	© Illustrated London News Ltd/Mary Evans
Picture No	11070335
Description	Gabrielle 'Coco' Chanel
Caption	A camera study of Gabrielle Bonheur, Coco Chanel (1883–1971).
Credit Line	© Illustrated London News Ltd/Mary Evans

Marion Hewlett Pike's pictures, copyright of Jeffie Pike Durham

Web Links, Archives and Videos consulted
Alan Riding: Ny Times: https://www.nytimes.com/2003/10/05/arts/art-jean-cocteau-before-his-own-fabulousness-consumed-him.html
Alexander palace.com: http://www.alexanderpalace.org/palace/Dmitri.html
Abbaye Aubazine website: http://abbaye.aubazine.com/?page_id=2.
Alice Casely-Hayford: Hunger TV: https://www.hungertv.com/feature/ten-ways-coco-chanel-changed-fashion/
Aubazine Documentair, L'abbaye d'Aubazine – Région Limousin – Le Monument Préféré des Français: https://www.youtube.com/watch?v=aiEy6WINix4
Balsan: http://www.balsan.fr/en/maison-balsan/depuis-1850/
Barbara Jones. The Enchanted Manor: www.theenchantedmanor.com/tag/coco-chanel-at-aubazine/
Beth Gersh-Nesic: thoughtco.com: https://www.thoughtco.com/picassos-women-183426
Britannica: https://www.britannica.com/place/Compiegne
Britannica: https://www.britannica.com/place/France/World-War-I
Britannica: https://www.britannica.com/topic/British-Expeditionary-Force
Britannica: https://www.britannica.com/event/World-War-I
British Empire: https://www.britishempire.co.uk/forces/20thhussarsgeorge barrow.htm
Britannica: https://www.britannica.com/biography/Nikolay-Rimsky-Korsakov
Britannica: https://www.britannica.com/biography/Igor-Stravinsky
Britannica: https://www.britannica.com/topic/British-Expeditionary-Force
Britannica: https://www.britannica.com/event/World-War-II
Britannica: https://www.britannica.com/biography/Jean-Cocteau

Britannica: https://www.britannica.com/biography/Cristobal-Balenciaga
Britannica: https://www.britannica.com/biography/Elsa-Schiaparelli
Britannica: https://www.britannica.com/biography/Paul-Poiret\
Biography: https://www.biography.com/people/christian-dior-9275315
Biography: https://www.biography.com/people/rasputin-9452162
Biography: https://www.biography.com/people/yves-saint-laurent-9469669
Biography: https://www.biography.com/people/coco-chanel-9244165
Catholic Saint. https://catholicsaints.info/saint-stephen-of-obazine/
Cath Pount: BBC.com: http://www.bbc.com/culture/story/20171106-the-rise-and-fall-of-fashions-greatest-innovator
Culture Chanel: http://culture.chanel.com/en/the-exhibition-visit/invisible-messages/jean-cocteau#top
Colin Mc Dowell: Business of Fashion: https://www.businessoffashion.com/articles/education/cristobal-balenciaga-1895-1972
Colin Mc Dowell: http://www.colinmcdowell.com/directory/thedirectory/directory-paul/poiret.html
Chanel: chanel.com
chanel.com: https://www.chanel.com/en_GB/fashion/news/2011/02/31-rue-cambon-the-story-behind-the-facade.html
Churchill Archives Centre. Churchill College. Storey's Way, Cambridge, CB3 0DS
Copyrights in Winston Churchill's own works are administered on behalf of the Churchill Estate by Curtis Brown Haymarket House, 28-29 Haymarket, London SW1Y 4SP.
Claude Delay, youtube interview: https://www.youtube.com/watch?v=jUaXu-BXoH0
Culture Chanel: http://culture.chanel.com/en/the-exhibition-visit/invisible-messages
http://culture.chanel.com/en/the-exhibition-visit
Coco Before Chanel (2009). Produced by Arnal, S., Benjo, C., Carcassonne, P., Delville, P., Lemal,G., Lippens, A., Scotta, C. Optimum Releasing.
Coco Chanel & Igor Stravinsky (2009). Produced by Chris Bolzli
Claudie Ossard,Veronika Zonabend.
Dana Thomas: Ny Times: https://www.nytimes.com/2002/02/24/magazine/the-power-behind-the-cologne.html
Enid Nemy: Ny Times: https://www.nytimes.com/1996/03/07/world/marie-helene-de-rothschild-65-worldly-hostess-extraordinaire.html
Five Minute History:http://fiveminutehistory.com/10-fascinating-facts-about-the-belle-epoque/?cn-reloaded=1
France Voyage: https://www.france-voyage.com/tourism/vichy-1744.htm
France This Way: https://www.francethisway.com/places/compiegne.php
Fondation Igor Stravinsky: https://fondation-igor-stravinsky.org/en/composer/biography/

Gabriella Asaro: Histoire Image: https://www.histoire-image.org/fr/etudes/splendeurs-miseres-courtisane-emilienne-alencon

Gabriella Asaro: Historie Image: https://www.histoire-image.org/fr/etudes/liane-pougy-charme-ambiguite-belle-epoque

Gallerease: https://gallerease.com/en/artists/paul-iribe__b048850799fc

Geni: https://www.geni.com/people/Diana-Wyndham-Countess-of-Westmorland/6000000015096288499

Geo Neo: Illustrator Lounge: https://illustratorslounge.com/fashion/fashion-fridays-paul-iribe-1883-1935

Gov UK: https://www.gov.uk/government/history/past-prime-ministers/winston-churchill

Helen Wigham:Vogue: https://www.vogue.co.uk/article/karl-lagerfeld

Histoire du travail des enfants en France. http://www.rhsansfrontieres.org/fr/domaines-d-intervention/lutte-contre-le-travail-des-enfants/19-domaines-d-intervention/lutte-contre-le-travail-des-enfants/302-histoire-du-travail-des-enfants-en-france

Isabelle Cerboneschi: all-i-c.com: https://all-i-c.com/gabrielle-chanel/

Katie Wignal: Lookup: https://lookup.london/coco-chanel-westminster-lamppost/

Kathleen Flood: vice.com: https://www.vice.com/en_uk/article/78wm39/original-creators-jean-cocteau

Janet Flanner: New Yorker: https://www.newyorker.com/magazine/1931/03/14/31-rue-cambon-2

Jennifer Latson:Time: http://time.com/3994196/coco-chanel-1883/

Jean Cocteau: https://www.jeancocteau.net/bio2_en.php

Jennifer Dunning: Ny Times: https://www.nytimes.com/1986/12/17/obituaries/serge-lifar-81-is-dead-shaper-of-french-ballet.html

Joanna Ling: Sothebys: https://www.sothebys.com/en/articles/cecil-beaton-and-the-exhibition-that-changed-photography-forever

Josh Jones: Open Culture: http://www.openculture.com/2017/05/the-1917-ballet-parade-created-by-erik-satie-pablo-picasso-jean-cocteau.html

Joseph Beuys:Tate: https://www.tate.org.uk/art/art-terms/a/avant-garde

Julia Neel: Vogue: https://www.vogue.co.uk/gallery/coco-chanel-quotes-and-photos

Justine Picardie: Fashion telegraph: http://fashion.telegraph.co.uk/news-features/TMG7986854/Coco-Chanel-at-war.html

Lanvin: https://www.lanvin.com/us/maison/history/

Layla Ilchi : WWD: https://wwd.com/fashion-news/fashion-scoops/karl-lagerfeld-dies-famous-quotes-1202985801/

La Rousse: Boulangisme. https://www.larousse.fr/encyclopedie/divers/boulangisme/28180

Locations: https://locations.filmfrance.net/fr/location/chateau-de-l-abbaye-de-royallieu-compiegne

Lonely planet: https://www.lonelyplanet.com/france/southwestern-france/biarritz

Mallen: Jesuit: https://www.jesuit.org.uk/blog/archives-look-records-mount-st-marys-college-and-other-jesuit-schools

Moulins. https://www.europeanbestdestinations.com/destinations/eden/moulins/

Michele Majer: Fashion history: https://fashion-history.lovetoknow.com/fashion-history-eras/demimonde

Misia Queen of Paris: http://misia-queenofparis.com/biography/

Mtholyoke: https://www.mtholyoke.edu/courses/rschwart/hist255-s01/boheme/dandyism.html

Musee Ysl Paris: https://museeyslparis.com/en/biography/mort-de-gabrielle-chanel

Normandie: http://en.normandie-tourisme.fr/discover/normandy-must-sees/the-10-top-normandy-must-sees/deauville-180-2.html

Ny Times: https://www.nytimes.com/1964/12/07/archives/mrs-balsan-dies-former-vanderhill.html

Ny Times: https://timesmachine.nytimes.com/timesmachine/1914/03/15/100303229.pdf

Pablo Picasso: https://www.pablopicasso.org/

Penguin Random House: https://www.penguinrandomhouse.com/books/243309/the-allure-of-chanel-by-paul-morand/9781782273677/

Penguin Random House: https://www.penguinrandomhouse.com/books/243309/the-allure-of-chanel-by-paul-morand/9781782273677/

Perfume Projects: http://www.perfumeprojects.com/museum/perfumers/ErnestBeaux.php

Quotes Wise: http://www.quoteswise.com/coco-chanel-quotes-3.html

Rai: http://www.letteratura.rai.it/articoli/marcel-proust-secondo-paul-morand/6782/default.aspx

Rhonda Garelick: The cut.com: https://www.thecut.com/2019/02/karl-lagerfeld-gabrielle-coco-chanel.html

Scotland People: https://www.scotlandspeople.gov.uk/article/coco-chanel-and-duke-westminster-highlands

Social Sciences: https://socialsciences.mcmaster.ca/econ/ugcm/3ll3/see/18thCentury.pdf

Serge Lifar: https://www.sergelifar.org/en/biography/the-french-period/

Stonyhurst: https://www.stonyhurst.ac.uk/wp-content/uploads/2014/04/SH_A-brief-history.pdf

Susan Irvine: Fashion Telegraph: http://fashion.telegraph.co.uk/news-features/TMG10275681/The-mysterious-Cristobal-Balenciaga.html

Telegraph: https://www.telegraph.co.uk/news/obituaries/6455125/Lady-Lindsay-of-Dowhill.html

Tina Sutton: The Making of Markova: https://themakingofmarkova.com/2013/05/01/coco-chanel-and-the-ballets-russes/

Tijana Radeska: The Vintage News: https://www.thevintagenews.com/2016/09/09/priority-pink-chanel-suit-worn-jacqueline-kennedy-stained-blood-will-placed-public-display-2103/

VAM: http://collections.vam.ac.uk/item/O1302355/coco-costume-design-beaton-cecil-sir/

Vogue: https://www.vogue.co.uk/article/coco-and-igor

Vogue: https://www.vogue.com.au/fashion/news/karl-on-chanels-legacy/news-story/b4a29891f45c37bd8a2791b54a4929af